# MAXIMIZE
## YOUR
# MULTIPLE

The Business Owner's Guide to the
Institutional Money Deal™

Jon Taylor

For entrepreneurs
looking to build and
sell their businesses for
MAXIMUM VALUE

Maximize Your Multiple: The Business Owner's Guide to the Institutional Money Deal™

Published by:
Stanton Park Capital
867 Boylston Street
5th Floor
Boston, MA 02116

The information and views contained in this book is provided for informational purposes only. It is not to be construed as an offer to buy or sell or a solicitation of an offer to buy or sell any financial instruments or to participate in any particular trading strategy. The information contained herein is believed to be reliable but the author makes no representation as to the accuracy or completeness of such information. Jonathan Taylor and/or his affiliates may be market makers or specialists in, act as advisers or lenders to, have positions in and effect transactions in securities of companies mentioned herein and also may provide, may have provided, or may seek to provide investment banking services for those companies. In addition, Jonathan Taylor and/or its affiliates or their respective officers, directors and employees may hold long or short positions in the securities, options thereon or other related financial products of companies discussed herein. The financial instruments discussed in this report may not be suitable for all investors, and investors must make their own investment decisions using their own independent advisors as they believe necessary and based upon their specific financial situations and investment objectives.

First Stanton Park Capital paperback edition April 2019

Taylor, Jonathan

ISBN # 9781513649658

# CONTENTS

I dedicate this book to my wife, Jami, who always inspires me to be my best.

# FOREWORD

Maximize Your Multiple by Jon Taylor is intended to help you understand what it takes to build and sell a business with significant value. If you want to be one of the few who achieves big successes in this area, this book is for you. You can learn a tremendous amount about building a successful business from this book. Every page is chock full of useful information. This book will encourage you to raise your business standards, challenge your limiting beliefs, develop a winning strategy and make the most of your time and efforts.

In this book:

- You will learn how the wealthiest people make their money
- You will explore what institutional investors look for in businesses
- You will understand how businesses are valued
- You will study how the institutional deal process works
- How you can avoid the 19 biggest mistakes business owners make
- You will learn how to build a scalable and profitable business
- You will understand how to develop the mindset of a winner

*Raymond Aaron*
*New York Bestselling Author*

# ACKNOWLEDGEMENTS

I would first like to thank my wife, Jami Taylor, without whom this book would not have been possible. Her excellent editing skills and support have been a very important part of this project.

I would also like to thank my children, Jack, Lauren, and Caroline, who inspire me to do my best and live a life with purpose and meaning.

## Bonus #1:

### FREE ONE-HOUR COACHING SESSION

The purchase of this book includes a free one-hour consultation with me, Jon Taylor. Please go to www.maxmultiple.com and register to get your free consultation. You can also contact my office at 888-314-7767 or jon@maxmultiple.com.

## Bonus #2:

### ADDITIONAL CONTENT AND DOWNLOADS

The purchase of this book includes the following free downloads:

- Sample Confidential Information Memorandum
- Sample Management Presentation
- Sample Asset Purchase Agreement
- Discounted Cash Flow Model
- Leveraged Buyout Model

Please go to www.maxmultiple.com and register to get these downloads.

You can also contact my office at 888-314-7767 or jon@maxmultiple.com.

# PREFACE

've been an investment banker for nearly 20 years, providing merger and acquisition and private equity advisory services to growing businesses in various industries. I've raised approximately two billion dollars in capital in the consumer products, technology, media, business services, and industrial products sectors.

My typical investor-clients are large corporations, commercial banks, and institutional investment funds (private equity firms) that want to invest in growing companies with significant profitability and cash flow. These investors represent literally trillions of dollars in equity and debt capital and account for the largest pile of money ever assembled in the history of the world. These are the proverbial "money masters of the universe" who search for high-quality businesses in which to invest.

In 2017, corporations and institutional investors spent $1.8 trillion buying 10,465 businesses in the United States alone. This is serious money for serious business owners who worked hard to build leading companies in many industries and market segments. By June of 2017, private equity firms in the U.S. and Europe had $848.3 billion in capital to deploy on acquisitions and buyouts. Leveraged two times, this represents $1.7 trillion in buying power -- the largest amount of cash ever accumulated by these funds.

**Below is a table illustrating the accumulation of these funds since 2005.**

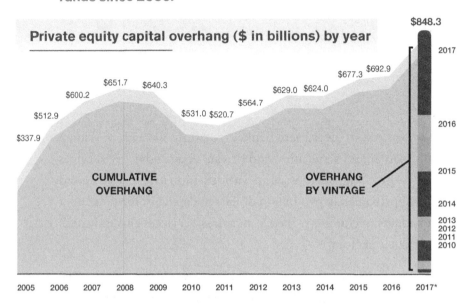

Private equity capital overhang ($ in billions) by year

$848.3

$677.3 $692.9

$651.7 $640.3

$600.2

$629.0 $624.0

$512.9

$564.7

$531.0 $520.7

$337.9

CUMULATIVE OVERHANG

OVERHANG BY VINTAGE

2017
2016
2015
2014
2013
2012
2011
2010

2005  2006  2007  2008  2009  2010  2011  2012  2013  2014  2015  2016  2017*

While these figures are impressive, the value of U.S. businesses is many times greater. The Exit Planning Institute (EPI), an organization dedicated to business succession planning, estimates that 4.5 million firms representing more than $10 trillion in business value will transition ownership over the next decade.

I have tremendous admiration and respect for entrepreneurs who carve out exciting businesses in highly competitive industries without the benefit of abundant capital, well-known brand names, and large workforces while facing powerful rivals. Their life experiences and "war" stories are fascinating.

However, one of my biggest frustrations as an investment banker for nearly two decades is the limited number of businesses and entrepreneurs I'm able to help. It's not that they don't want my help or that I don't want to help them. The simple reality is that most businesses aren't qualified for institutional capital -- primarily because they're too small to be interesting to the money masters of the universe.

Maybe you've heard a story like this before. A guy starts a business and quickly grows it to several million dollars in sales with ease. He then sells it for millions of dollars to a large corporation or investor, leaving him with more money than he'll ever need. He retires from the cares of the world and enjoys a lifestyle that includes expensive fancy homes, dream vacations, and exotic cars.

That story is a lie. The vast majority of businesses will never come anywhere close to $1 million dollars in sales and a lucrative exit. Moreover, talented and hard-working people who build successful businesses usually aren't content to rest on their laurels for very long. According to the U.S. Census Bureau, 78.5 percent of businesses in 2010 had no employees whatsoever and less than $50,000 in sales. That's not exactly the picture of success suggested by the title "business owner."

Of course, in rare instances, entrepreneurs do achieve big money exits relatively quickly, but this is more like "catching lightning in a bottle" than achieving highly predictable results. The more interesting question is, why don't more businesses make it to the multi-million-dollar winners circle? Wouldn't you like to know? Wouldn't you like to be one of them? If not, this book isn't for you, and I suggest you put it down now.

According to EPI CEO and President Christopher Snider, only about 20 to 30 percent of businesses that go to market actually result in a sale. This means the clear majority of businesses will never sell and will most likely either be shut down or transferred for a nominal sum to someone else. This estimate is consistent with a report by BizBuySell, the leading online marketplace for businesses, which found that only about one in every five business listings on its online marketplace closed a transaction in 2016.

One in five. How do you like those odds? How would you like to spend 20 to 30 years building a business and then have only a 20-percent chance of selling it for any significant amount of money? Do those odds sound good to you? If you're sane, you'd say "no way." These aren't the odds that someone highly committed to success would accept. No, a success-minded business owner would look for any possible way to increase those odds significantly.

This book is about how to make the entrepreneur's dream of achieving the big money deal a reality. I've seen too many business owners plod away for decades with little to no hope of achieving a transaction that matches their dreams and innate potential.

So, this book is a warning cry to entrepreneurs and business owners who want more than ordinary results. It's about achieving extraordinary results for business owners who don't want to leave their success to dumb luck. This book is for owners who seek a proactive approach to building a valuable business that will generate significant wealth for themselves and others.

# CHAPTER 1

## Businesses Generate Tremendous Wealth

The majority of wealth on planet Earth today was created by businesses that offer products and services that people want. Think about the immense profits businesses like Apple, JP Morgan Chase, Google, and Microsoft generate year in and year out for their shareholders. In 2016, Fortune 500 companies made $890 billion in profits on $12 trillion in revenue. In January of 2018, the total value of publicly traded companies in the U.S. exceeded $30 trillion. These companies are valuable because people are willing to trade their hard-earned dollars for the products and services they provide. Customers willingly enter into transactions with these businesses because their products and services are considered to be more valuable than customers' money; otherwise, people wouldn't buy their products in the first place.

I don't mean to suggest that businesses like these don't make mistakes or morally questionable decisions from time to time. But on balance, these money-making businesses have done more than other institutions to create wealth and improve the living conditions of their shareholders, employees, and communities. Moreover, businesses have done much more to lift people out of poverty worldwide than governments, non-governmental organizations

(NGOs), and charitable organizations. Business owners can and should be proud of their legacy of service to humanity.

---

## The Wealthiest People in the World Own Businesses

Perhaps the best evidence of business-generated wealth is found by examining the world's wealthiest people and how they made their money. Every one of the top 100 individuals on the 2017 Forbes 400 list acquired wealth through business ownership. Here's a list of the top 20 individuals on the Forbes 400 list.

| Rank | Name | Net Worth | Source | Country |
|------|------|-----------|--------|---------|
| #1 | Bill Gates | $86 B | Microsoft | United States |
| #2 | Warren Buffett | $75.6 B | Berkshire Hathaway | United States |
| #3 | Jeff Bezos | $72.8 B | Amazon.com | United States |
| #4 | Amancio Ortega | $71.3 B | Zara | Spain |
| #5 | Mark Zuckerberg | $56 B | Facebook | United States |
| #6 | Carlos Slim Helu | $54.5 B | Grupo Carso | Mexico |
| #7 | Larry Ellison | $52.2 B | Oracle | United States |
| #8 | Charles Koch | $48.3 B | Koch Industries | United States |
| #8 | David Koch | $48.3 B | Koch Industries | United States |
| #10 | Michael Bloomberg | $47.5 B | Bloomberg LP | United States |
| #11 | Jim Walton | $38.4 B | Walmart | United States |
| #12 | S. Robson Walton | $38.3 B | Walmart | United States |
| #13 | Alice Walton | $38.2 B | Walmart | United States |
| #14 | Sheldon Adelson | $35.4 B | Las Vegas Sands | United States |
| #15 | Steve Ballmer | $33.6 B | Microsoft | United States |
| #16 | Jacqueline Mars | $25.5 B | Mars, Incorporated | United States |
| #16 | John Mars | $25.5 B | Mars, Incorporated | United States |
| #18 | Phil Knight | $25.2 B | Nike | United States |
| #19 | Michael Dell | $23.2 B | Dell | United States |

## Business Assets Generate the Most Income

The wealthiest people in the world teach us two big lessons. First, their net worth is directly related to the assets they own, not the salary they collect. They may own expensive homes, yachts, and other toys, but the bulk of their wealth is invested in business assets that produce income. The second lesson is that they hold their business assets for many years, indicating a compounding effect that occurs through asset ownership over time.

IRS income data indicate wealth is derived from business assets, not salaries and wages. Of the top 400 earners in the U.S. from 2009, less than 10 percent of their total income came from salaries and wages. In fact, the bulk of it -- nearly 84 percent -- came from business or asset ownership. Almost half of their income derived from capital gains on the sale of businesses or assets, and 35 percent as earned from partnerships, corporations, and dividends. Therefore, business assets generated more than eight times more income for high-income individuals than salaries and wages alone. The lesson here is clear: Americans with the highest incomes owe the bulk of their income to owning businesses and other income-producing assets that increase in value over time. Below is a breakdown of income by source for the top 400 earners in the U.S. in 2009.

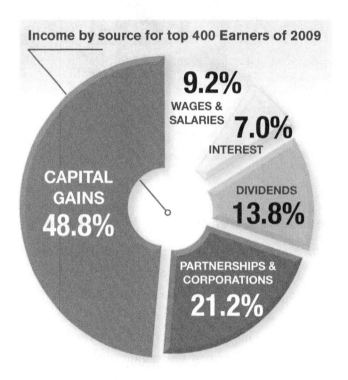

**Income by source for top 400 Earners of 2009**

9.2%
WAGES & SALARIES

7.0%
INTEREST

CAPITAL GAINS
48.8%

DIVIDENDS
13.8%

PARTNERSHIPS & CORPORATIONS
21.2%

If the connection between business ownership and wealth still isn't clear to you, here's additional convincing data: According to research by CEG Worldwide, business ownership is the norm among 33 percent of affluent individuals (investable assets between $1 million to $5 million), 74.5 percent of super-affluent individuals (investable assets between $5 million to $25 million), and 90 percent of ultra-affluent individuals (investable assets over $25 million). The wealthier one is, the more likely one is to own a business, which is what most super-affluent and ultra-affluent individuals do.

**Business Ownership %**

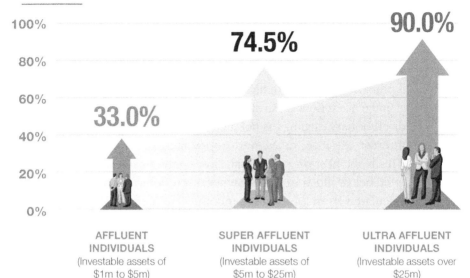

| | | |
|:--:|:--:|:--:|
| **AFFLUENT INDIVIDUALS** (Investable assets of $1m to $5m) | **SUPER AFFLUENT INDIVIDUALS** (Investable assets of $5m to $25m) | **ULTRA AFFLUENT INDIVIDUALS** (Investable assets over $25m) |

## Business Ownership Concentrates Time and Money

Logically, it makes sense that business ownership leads to the greatest gains in wealth because business owners are focusing both their time and their money to create wealth for themselves. While they take on the most risk, they also receive the greatest reward. People who work for a salary are only investing their time and have limited upside potential because they have relatively little-to-no "skin in the game." Likewise, passive investors who are only investing money and aren't actively involved in day-to-day business operations have a limited upside as well. Consequently, passive investors aren't well-positioned to substantially grow the value of the business over time by making the appropriate operational decisions and doing the required work. Clearly, active business ownership provides one of the best opportunities to build wealth over time.

## Few Businesses Generate Significant Wealth

Although businesses have the potential to create significant wealth for their owners, the reality is that quite few businesses actually do. According to IRS tax data from 2013, only about 3 percent of the 5.9 million active corporations in the U.S had average discretionary earnings of $1 million or more. (We define discretionary earnings as net income, plus officer compensation, interest expense, taxes, and depreciation and amortization.) This is the best proxy for cash flow to the business owner. The table below illustrates how owner discretionary earnings can be calculated from a business's income statement.

### Sample Income Statement

| | |
|---|---|
| Revenue | $10,000,000 |
| Cost of sales | $7,000,000 |
| Gross profit | $3,000,000 |
| | |
| Sales, general & administrative expense | $2,400,000 |
| **Operating profit** | **$600,000** |
| | |
| Add back: owner salary | $50,000 |
| Add back: interest expense | $100,000 |
| Add back: depreciation & amortization | $250,000 |
| **Owner Discretionary Earnings** | **$1,000,000** |

On average, businesses with owner discretionary earnings of at least $1 million have annual sales volume of $10 million or more. The scale and profitability of these businesses make them exceptionally valuable to their owners. Unfortunately, most business owners -- although they may work hard, be highly skilled in their trade, and be great people overall -- likely will fail to create the kind of wealth required to leave a substantial legacy.

How is this possible? Aren't most business owners rich? Unfortunately, the data prove otherwise. According to IRS data, 57.2 percent of businesses had average incomes of $48,000 or less. That's less than the median U.S. household income of $59,039 in 2016. This means most business owners put most of their net worth on the line only to earn an income that is below the national average. How crazy is that?

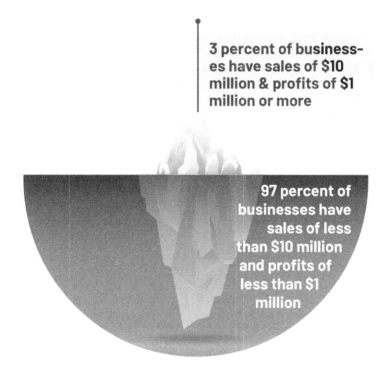

3 percent of business-es have sales of $10 million & profits of $1 million or more

97 percent of businesses have sales of less than $10 million and profits of less than $1 million

How is it that the few who do achieve significant business success do it? Do the top 3 percent of business owners have something others don't? Probably not in the traditional sense, you might think. For example, there are business owners worth tens and even hundreds of millions of dollars or more with limited education, age, experience, family wealth, or connections. Some might say these people are just "lucky". But as Charlie Munger, Warren Buffet's long-time business partner has said, "To get what you want, you have to deserve what you want. The world is not yet a crazy enough place to reward a whole bunch of undeserving people." You must do many things correctly to build a successful business, so the idea that dumb luck plays a significant role is somewhat foolish.

One of the best ways to understand how to create a valuable business is to consider the characteristics of institutional caliber businesses and the people who build them. Institutional investor-backed businesses include the largest and most successful businesses in the world, like Apple and Google, as well as privately-held, private equity-backed businesses you may not have ever heard of. Whether public or private, institutional investors have rather stringent criteria for the companies in which they invest. In the following chapter, we'll look closer at institutional investors and some of their basic investment criteria.

# CHAPTER 2

## Is Your Company an Institutional Money Deal Candidate?

Y ou might be asking yourself, what kind of business do I need to create to gain significant affluence or wealth? The answer is relatively simple: You need a business that generates earnings of at least $1 million or more. Why $1 million? Great question! The answer is that businesses that breach the $1 million profit threshold have achieved "institutional scale." When a business has institutional scale, it is large enough to be interesting to many institutional investors as a potential investment.

### Who Are Institutional Investors?

Institutional investors include high net worth individuals and families, large corporations, private equity funds, banks, insurance companies, pension funds, hedge funds, investment advisors, endowment funds, and mutual funds. In other words, institutional investors control immense sums of money and hire some of the smartest, best-educated, and hardest-working people to invest it for them.

As of 2019, some of the better-known institutional investment groups include Blackstone ($439 billion), the Carlyle Group ($210 billion), Texas Pacific Group ($84 billion), Kohlberg Kravis Roberts ($191 billion), Apollo Global Management ($269 billion), and Bain Capital ($95 billion). These investors control literally trillions of dollars in assets and are always looking for the next "deal" to invest in. In other words, there is a vast ocean of cash available to entrepreneurs who build successful businesses that can attract the attention of these groups.

In the last few decades, institutional investors have been allocating more and more capital to invest in privately owned businesses with the goal of generating significant returns on their money. The main reason is that this is where most of the growth and innovation happens, and the relative purchase prices for these enterprises are usually lower than those in the public markets.

As a business owner, you need to know that more money exists to make your dreams come true than has ever existed in the history of mankind. The age of the entrepreneur has arrived, and massive piles of cash have been accumulated to shower on the successful entrepreneur.

## Institutional Investors Represent Trillions of Dollars in Capital

As of June 2017, more than one trillion dollars in committed capital sat in the coffers of private equity and venture capital funds worldwide. Over $1.1 trillion in commitments is available for drawdown by fund managers — $145.4 billion allotted to venture capital and $961.5 billion to private equity. Public companies, valued at over $30 trillion in the United States alone, are often highly acquisitive as well. In total, institutional investors spent $1.8 trillion to buy 10,465 businesses in the United States in 2017.

## What Kind of Businesses Do Institutional Investors Look For?

What does it take for a business owner to attract institutional investor money? The first and most important thing to understand is that institutional investors do big deals, not small deals. For institutional investors, bigger is always better. That said, institutional investors seek businesses in nearly every industry you can imagine. Let's discuss specific deal criteria to give you some sense of size and scale.

On the low end, and by this I mean some of the smallest institutional money deals happening these days, a private company needs to have at least $1 million in annual profits -- earnings before interest, taxes, depreciation, and amortization (EBITDA). And that's just to get some consideration. To really put your company in the running for big investment, you'll want to have $5 million to $10 million or more in EBITDA.

## How Are Private Equity Funds Structured?

Let's explore why a company with $1 million in profits starts to matter to institutional investors. Institutional investors and corporations manage hundreds of millions and billions of dollars in assets at a time. So, let's say you're a private equity fund managing $100 million in assets -- a relatively small fund by today's standards. $100 million in assets will generate about $2 million in annual management fees (2% of assets under management is typical), so you're looking at a budget that might hire 5 to 10 investment professionals.

With a team this size, you probably won't have the ability to effectively manage more than, say, 20 investments, because for each one, you have monthly and quarterly reporting, quarterly board meetings to attend, regular limited partner letters and communication to manage, new investment opportunities to explore, previous investments to exit, and new funds to raise.

Twenty investments dictate an average check size of $5 million. A $5 million equity check with $3 million of debt implies a company value of $8 million. $8 million in company value implies average company profits of $1.3 million to $2 million, because 4x to 6x are typical profit multiples for businesses in this size range. The table below illustrates this concept.

| | |
|---|---|
| Equity Value | $5,000,000 |
| Debt Value | $3,000,000 |
| **Company Value (Enterprise Value)** | **$8,000,000** |
| | |
| Purchase Multiple (Company Value / Profit) | 6.0x |
| **Implied Profit (Company Value / Purchase Multiple)** | **$1,333,333** |

I talk to businesses owners every day who either want to sell their companies to or raise capital from institutional investors. Most of them are convinced their businesses are perfect for institutional investors and that they would make ideal partners. Likewise, most business owners I know are passionate about what they do, speak enthusiastically about their business's products, brand, accomplishments, market opportunities, and growth potential. However, what many of these business owners fail to understand is that institutional investors couldn't care less about these things if the company hasn't achieved significant scale and profitability.

## What About Unprofitable Tech Companies That Sell for Big Money?

Sure, there are some tech companies that sell "vaporware" for millions of dollars, but typically these types of deals are exceptions to the rule. I know that someone reading this right now might be saying, "But I know so and so who sold his business for millions, and he wasn't close to making a profit of any kind." While it's true that a relatively small number of businesses in select industries (usually science or technology-related with significant potential for disruptive innovation) with little to no profit do achieve institutional scale investments or exits, these instances are relatively rare.

## What Kind of Returns Do Institutional Investors Require?

Let's explore some of the other key criteria institutional investors consider when they invest in businesses. One key characteristic is their desire for big returns on their money. In fact, many institutional equity investors target annual returns of 30 percent or more. "Whoa," you might say, "that sounds really high." But understand this: These investors typically achieve these returns with leverage. They use significant amounts of debt, usually about 50 percent of the purchase price, and buy only well-run businesses in industries that have significant growth potential.

Beyond leverage, the primary strategy institutional investors use is buying these businesses as cheaply as possible. As a result, the return requirements dictate a purchase price of 6 times EBITDA or less in many cases, because this equates to an unlevered return of 16.6% per annum, since the inverse of the purchase multiple (1 divided by 6) equals 16.6%. Now, if you buy the business with 50% equity and 50% debt, your return on equity is now "magically" increased to 33.3 percent, because 1 divided by 3 equals 33.3 percent. This table illustrates the concept.

| | Unleveraged Investment | Leveraged Investment |
|---|---|---|
| Company Purchase Price | $12,000,000 | $12,000,000 |
| Equity Investment | $12,000,000 | $6,000,000 |
| Debt Investment | $0 | $6,000,000 |
| Annual EBITDA | $2,000,000 | $2,000,000 |
| Return on Equity | 16.6% (2,000,000 / 12,000,000) | 33.3% (2,000,000 / 6,000,000) |

## What Else Do Institutional Investors Look For?

Other key criteria institutional investors use to buy businesses are:

1. Strong management team in place

2. Limited customer concentration (no single customer accounting for more than say 30 percent to 40 percent of sales).

3. High profit margin (usually 10 percent or more).

4. Significant competitive differentiation (unique strengths and/or strategies relative to competition).

5. Growth opportunities (either organic or through acquisitions).

6. Product offerings that are not too trendy or cyclical.

## Strong Management Teams Required

In most cases, institutional investors want businesses that already have strong management teams in place to run the company once they invest in or acquire it. This is because institutional investors don't typically operate businesses. In most cases, they're looking to simply back existing management teams and rely on them to manage the daily operations and execute the company's long-term strategy. Of course, institutional investors want board representation and periodic reports on the company's financial results and progress, typically on a monthly or quarterly basis.

## Limited Customer Concentration

Institutional investors want companies with a relatively diversified customer base that are perceived to be less risky than companies with significant customer concentration. For example, if a company sells widgets to Wal-Mart, and Wal-Mart accounts for 45 percent of its sales, the company's survival likely would be seriously jeopardized if Walmart were to switch to another widget supplier because nearly half of this company's sales could disappear overnight.

Of course, it varies by industry and company, but when a customer reaches 20 percent or more of total sales, the business owner should be thinking about the potential risks this customer represents. For example, how would the business be affected if the customer started buying from another supplier or went bankrupt without warning? This happens more often than you might think. What separates extraordinary businesses from ordinary businesses is being mindful of and planning for contingencies like these.

## High Profit Margins

Most investors want to avoid businesses with low-profit margins. Why? Because there's less "margin of safety" in a low-margin business. This is something Graham and Dodd talk about in detail in their legendary book, Security Analysis – a book that is essentially Warren Buffet's investing bible. If your business makes a 3 percent profit margin and something goes wrong, it can turn into a loss much more quickly than if you were making a 13 percent or 23 percent profit margin. High-profit businesses can afford to make some mistakes and still make money. Also, a low profit margin is an indication of a highly competitive market environment. Institutional investors don't like to invest in highly competitive and commoditized industries due to their inherent risk and lack of growth potential.

## Competitive Differentiation

Competitive differentiation is an important consideration because it speaks to the long-term sustainability of the business. For example, if a business is no better at providing a good or service than its competitors either more cheaply or with higher quality, it likely will have difficulty achieving sustained growth and profitability over the long term. Companies with strong competitive differentiation might have proprietary offerings, strong branding, technical expertise, lower cost structure, high product quality, and/or significant scale that is not easily duplicated.

## Growth Opportunities

Institutional investors want businesses that have significant, profitable growth opportunities because growth means their investment's value will increase over time. These growth opportunities might include increasing the profitability of its existing line of business, winning new customers, introducing new products or services, and acquiring complementary businesses. Profitable growth is important because increased profits mean increased business value, and increased business value means investors make more money.

So as you can see, institutional investors are rather picky about their business investments. While some of their considerations relate to the practicality and the economics of their business models, many point to the overall quality of the business themselves. If you're looking to sell your company to one of these investors, it's good to know what they are looking for. Your goal as a business owner should be to build the highest quality business possible, regardless of who might be the owner in the future.

## Greater Size Means Greater Value Per Dollar of Earnings

The rewards for accomplishing this are significant. Larger, more profitable business are worth two to three times more per dollar of earnings than businesses with average or even somewhat above average earnings. Below is a table showing valuation multiples for businesses with average to above average profitability compared to businesses with annual earnings of $5 million or more. On average, the more profitable businesses sell for owner discretionary earnings multiples 2.9 times higher than the "average" business. Likewise, revenue multiples, return on assets, and return on equity metrics are all two to three times those of the smaller companies.

| Valuation Multiple | Owner Discretionary Earnings of $50K to $250K | Owner Discretionary Earnings of $5 million or more | Difference |
|---|---|---|---|
| Firm Value / Net Sales | 0.5x | 0.9x | 1.9x |
| Firm Value / EBITDA | 4.5x | 6.7x | 1.5x |
| Firm Value / Discretionary Earnings | 2.3x | 6.7x | 2.9x |
| Firm Value / Book Value | 2.2x | 3.6x | 1.6x |
| Return on Assets | 16% | 32.5% | 2.0x |
| Return on Equity | 26% | 71% | 2.7x |

# CHAPTER 3

## Business Valuation Basics

This chapter is a quick primer on business valuation. As I explain in more detail later, I strongly recommend that all business owners have a valuation done every one to two years. A valuation is comparable to a check-up at the doctor's office. It gauges the health of the business overall and can bring to light areas of strength and weakness. A valuation also surfaces certain risk factors that can curtail your ability to maximize your multiple down the road.

When my firm prepares a valuation, we review the history, financial condition and operating results of the Company. We also study the competitive environment, industry outlook, economic climate, and the company specific risks. This composite approach—an analysis of both the intrinsic business and the market context—generates a clear view of the value of the business as the marketplace would determine it at a given point in time.

In the sections that follow, I outline the key aspects of the valuation exercise, including common valuation terms and practices. Business owners who are diligently tracking the value of their enterprises through consistent, yearly valuations can safely skip this content. Most business owners, however, would benefit from knowing how a valuation is done. This knowledge can empower you to secure your own regular valuations. From the information they generate, you can know precisely how and where to build value toward maximizing your multiple at exit. So, let's dive in:

## Fair Market Value Definition

Fair market value is defined as the cash price at which property would change hands between a willing buyer and seller. In other words, the value of a business should be understood in the context of what someone is willing to pay for it in a market-based transaction. Fair market value is the most common valuation standard and is often dictated by federal or state law.

## Components of Enterprise Value

Enterprise value or firm value represents the sum of the market value of debt and equity invested in a business. You can think of enterprise value as the purchase price or market value of a house which is very different than homeowner's equity that is derived by subtracting the mortgage balance from the market value of the home. In business valuation, you typically add cash to the company's equity value (or subtract it from the debt balance to calculate net debt) because this is the business owner's money. Below is a chart that illustrates this concept.

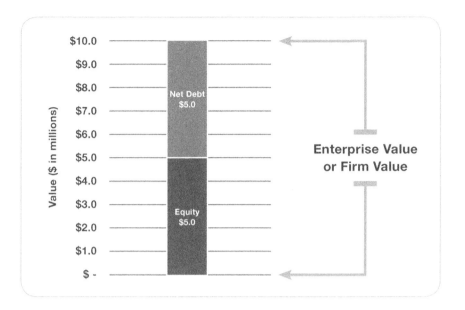

## Buyers Buy Cash Flow

The primary benefit business buyers receive when they acquire a business is the underlying cash flows it generates business. The best proxy for cash flow to the buyer is earnings before interest, taxes, depreciation, and amortization or "EBITDA". This represents the cash flow to the owner of the business before they pay interest on outstanding debt and income taxes. Depreciation and amortization are non-cash charges generated from fixed or intangible asset purchases that occurred in the past but are deducted from current or future income.

## Adjustments to EBITDA

EBITDA is usually adjusted so that it reflects the "true" economic earnings of the business, so discretionary, non-recurring or nonoperating expenses are added back. Common adjustments to EBITDA include the following:

- excess shareholder compensation,
- personal auto expenses,
- non-business-related expenses,
- non-recurring legal or litigation expenses,
- business relocation expenses,
- owner life insurance premiums,
- country clubs dues,
- compensation to non-working family members or friends, and
- excessive inventory write-offs.

## What is a Multiple?

Let's talk about multiples next. A multiple is essentially the inverse of a return on investment calculation. So, for example, if we pay a five multiple on the earnings of a company, we're effectively getting a 20 percent return (1 / 5 = 0.20), because it will take five years to recoup our initial investment. Multiples vary by a number of factors including company size, industry, growth rate, profitability, risk profile, and availability of credit. EBITDA multiples are the most common business valuation metric because it allows for easy comparison of alternative investment opportunities.

## Three Approaches to Valuation

There are generally three acceptable methods for valuing a

company – (1) market, (2) income, and (3) asset. The asset approach to valuation is normally only used when the subject company does not appear to be able to continue operations as a going-concern or when the company is expected to be liquidated. This might be because it is insolvent or will be shutdown.

This approach can be very complex and time consuming due to the fact that it requires an appraisal of all assets and liabilities, tangible and intangible, of the business. Therefore, it is not used normally in conjunction with the appraisal of an operating business that is anticipated to carry on as a going concern.

The market approach uses the values of similar businesses that are sold on public stock exchanges or private business sales to other companies or investor groups, otherwise known as mergers and acquisitions, to approximate the value of a business. The income approach looks at the earnings and return on investment a business will generate in the future, and discounts those earnings back to the present at a discount rate appropriate for the specific subject company.

## Comparable Public Company Method

With the comparable public company method, we look at how a group of similar publicly traded companies are valued. In this case, we're trying to value a consumer electronics business, so we've pulled relevant statistics from several publicly traded consumer electronics companies. As you can see, the firm value to revenue and EBITDA multiples for Apple, Samsung, Sony, Philips, Hewlett-Packard, Panasonic, Motorola, Toshiba, LG, and Asus varies. However, the median revenue and EBITDA multiples are 0.8 and 5.5. Now, if we're trying to use this multiple to value a relatively small private business, we should apply a significant discount, perhaps 30 percent to 40 percent due to the lack of marketability and illiquidity of privately-held shares compared to those of public traded shares. Also, you would typically add a control premium of perhaps 15 percent to 25 percent to publicly traded shares, because they represent minority or non-control ownership stakes in those businesses.

| Company Name | Enterprise Value | Total Revenue (TTM) | Normalized EBITDA (TTM) | EV / Revenue | EV / EBITDA |
|---|---|---|---|---|---|
| Apple | 1,084,285,856 | 255,274,000 | 78,327,000 | 4.2 | 13.8 |
| Samsung Electronics | 279,850,503 | 211,270,940 | 69,516,859 | 1.3 | 4.1 |
| Sony | 61,716,787 | 78,283,630 | 10,034,984 | 0.8 | 5.6 |
| Philips | 43,720,512 | 21,087,900 | 2,984,272 | 2.1 | 14.0 |
| Hewlett-Packard | 40,302,980 | 55,507,000 | 3,934,000 | 0.7 | 11.5 |
| Panasonic | 29,882,786 | 73,626,695 | 6,216,361 | 0.4 | 4.8 |
| Motorola Solutions | 25,063,727 | 6,829,000 | 1,724,000 | 3.7 | 14.9 |
| Toshiba | 8,392,615 | 40,012,270 | 3,250,752 | 0.2 | 2.6 |
| LG Electronics | 18,488,268 | 54,142,671 | 4,153,054 | 0.3 | 4.6 |
| ASUS | 3,641,686 | 13,977,928 | 674,729 | 0.3 | 5.4 |
| Mean | 159,534,572 | 81,001,203 | 18,081,601 | 1.4 | 8.1 |
| Median | 35,092,883 | 54,824,836 | 4,043,527 | 0.8 | 5.5 |

## Comparable Transaction Method

The precedent transaction method uses transaction data from the sale of similar businesses. Business transaction data can be found in news sources as well as proprietary databases like DealStats, CapitalIQ, and Pitchbook. When relevant descriptive statistics are compiled, averaged and applied to the subject company's financial results, the result suggests implied value for the business. Below is a summary of 12 comparable transactions for a machine shop business. As you can see, the median revenue and EBITDA multiples is 0.71 and 3.79, respectively.

## Comparable Transaction Summary

| Business Description | Sale Date | Firm Value | Firm Value / Sales | Firm Value / EBITDA |
|---|---|---|---|---|
| Machine Shop | 06/29/2018 | $1,900,000 | 0.75x | 1.7x |
| Machine Shop | 06/08/2018 | $3,500,000 | 0.70x | 3.1x |
| Industrial Machine Shop | 05/20/2018 | $1,550,000 | 0.70x | 3.5x |
| Machine Shop | 01/02/2018 | $2,871,000 | 1.53x | 5.3x |
| Industrial C&C Machine Shop | 09/30/2017 | $1,600,000 | 0.72x | 3.7x |
| Machine Shop | 09/01/2017 | $3,375,964 | 1.41x | |
| Machine Shop | 12/29/2016 | $1,550,000 | 0.70x | 4.2x |
| Machine Shop | 09/13/2016 | $2,075,000 | 0.67x | |
| Machine Metal Finishing and Manufacturing Services | 05/05/2016 | $2,950,000 | 1.38x | 3.9x |
| Machine Shop | 04/18/2016 | $745,000 | 0.26x | |
| Computer Numerical Control (CNC) Machine Shop | | $1,500,000 | 0.75x | 9.2x |
| Precision Sheet Metal and Machined Parts Manufacturer | | $869,313 | 0.24x | |
| | | Mean | 0.82x | 4.33x |
| | | Median | 0.71x | 3.79x |

## Cost of Capital

The cost of capital is the expected market rate of return to attract funds for a particular investment. This rate of return, also called the "discount rate," reflects both time value of money and risk. The key question to address in the development of the discount rate is, "what is an appropriate rate of return to expect if the future cash flows to investment holders were purchased?"

When using the income approach to determine the enterprise value, it is important that the discount rates used are relevant and appropriate to the economic income being discounted. In particular, the "weighted average cost of capital" should be utilized when one is discounting the cash flows to all capital providers. The result of this calculation reflects the value of the entire investment to all stakeholders – both equity and long-term debt holders.

Not every company has the same capital structure. Some companies obtain more of their capital from borrowing than others who might obtain their capital from shareholder contributions. As stated above, using the enterprise value allows us to compare companies independent of their capital structures.

Accordingly, the related cost of capital to the enterprise value is the weighted average cost of capital (WACC), the weighted average of the combined cost of equity and after-tax cost of debt. To determine the WACC, we must first determine the company's cost of equity and after-tax cost of debt.

## Cost of Equity

The most common approach for determining the cost of equity

is the Capital Asset Pricing Model (CAPM). CAPM is based on the assumption that all businesses and business interests are a subset of the investment opportunities available in the total capital market. As a result, the relevant value of a business should theoretically be subject to the same economic forces and relationships that determine the values of other investment assets. Essentially, CAPM calculates the required or expected rate of return of a particular asset through a risk-free rate, a risk premium based on the associated risk of the asset, and a beta based on comparable public companies, which measures the volatility of the asset relative to the overall market. The CAPM formula is as follows:

**Return on asset = Risk free rate + Beta (Return on market – Risk free rate)**

We calculate the company's cost of equity using the following components:

- A risk-free rate we consider to be the 20-year U.S. Treasury Bond for which we typically use Duff & Phelps' normalized 20-year U.S. treasury yield.

- An appropriate industry Beta factor which reflects the riskiness of the company's specific industry as compared to the riskiness of the total stock market.

- An equity risk premium, which is the additional compensation for the increased risk that investors demand for investing in a broad index of the common stock market (such as the Standard & Poor's 500 Stock Composite Index).

- An additional premium determined by the size and specific risk factors of the subject company itself.

## ABC Company Weighted Average of Cost of Capital Analysis

### COST OF EQUITY:

| | |
|---|---:|
| Risk free rate (1) | 3.09% |
| Beta (2) | 1.37 |
| Equity risk premium (3) | 6.70% |
| Company size premium (4) | 11.65% |
| Company specific premium | 3.00% |
| ABC Company cost of equity (5) | 26.92% |

### COST OF DEBT:

| | |
|---|---:|
| Pretax cost of debt | 5.84% |
| Tax rate | 30.00% |
| After tax cost of debt | 4.09% |

### WEIGHTED AVERAGE COST OF CAPITAL:

| | |
|---|---:|
| Debt-to-equity ratio | 20.00% |
| Weighted Average Cost of Capital (WACC) | 22.35% |

(1) 20-year treasury rate - Duff & Phelps normalized rate

(2) Industry beta - Duff & Phelps Cost of Capital Navigator

(3) Equity Risk Premium - Duff & Phelps normalized equity risk premium

(4) Size premium - CRSP 10Z decile

(5) Based on CAPM [risk free rate + beta * (return on market - risk free rate)]

## Discounted Cash Flow Method

The discounted cash flow method requires that the company's management estimate future free cash flow which is the cash that is available to be paid out to the invested capital holders of the business without jeopardizing the Company's future operations. This requires management to make certain assumptions about the Company's growth rates and profit margins, capital expenditures, and working capital necessary to support the earning generating capacity of the business. Below is a three-year discounted cash flow model output based on a 22.4 percent discount rate. As you can see, the company's anticipated cash flow discounted at 22.4 percent results in a firm value of $5.5 million.

**ABC Company Discounted Cash Flow Analysis** (figures in US dollars)

| | PROJECTED FYE DECEMBER 31: | | |
| --- | --- | --- | --- |
| | 2020P | 2021P | 2022P |
| Net Income | $1,000,000 | $1,100,000 | $1,210,000 |
| Net Interest Expense / (Income) | 100,000 | 100,000 | 100,000 |
| Marginal Tax Rate | 30.0% | 30.0% | 30.0% |
| Financing Tax Shield | (30,000) | (30,000) | (30,000) |
| Earnings Before Interest | $1,070,000 | $1,170,000 | $1,280,000 |
| Depreciation & Amortization | (80,000) | (80,000) | (80,000) |
| Earnings Before Interest, Depreciation & Amortization | $990,000 | $1,090,000 | $1,200,000 |
| Less: Change in Net Working Capital | (100,000) | (110,000) | (121,000) |
| Less: Capital Expenditures | (80,000) | (80,000) | (80,000) |
| Unlevered Free Cash Flow | $810,000 | $900,000 | $999,000 |
| Discount Rate | 22.4% | | |
| Present Value of Unlevered Free Cash Flow | $662,035 | $601,222 | $545,448 |
| Growth Rate | 3.0% | | |
| Terminal EBITDA | $1,965,829 | | |
| Terminal Value | $10,159,321 | | |
| Present Value of Terminal Value | $3,705,483 | | |
| Sum of Present Value of Unlevered Free Cash Flow | $1,808,706 | | |
| Enterprise Value | $5,514,188 | | |
| Net Debt | $1,000,000 | | |
| Equity Value | $4,514,188 | | |

## Leveraged Buyout Method

The leveraged buyout method calculates the return on equity and debt investments made in a business over a five to seven period given a certain set of financial projections and purchase price assumptions today. With this method, it is common to assume that approximately 40 percent to 50 percentage of the purchase price is financed with debt. This leverage increases the return on equity because it reduces the amount of equity required to purchase the business. This is the most common method used by private equity firms to price businesses. In this model output below, we see that the equity investment yields a 32.7 percentage annualized return in 2023 assuming a 6.0x exit multiple.

| Key Inputs & Assumptions | | | Outputs | | | |
|---|---|---|---|---|---|---|
| Company Name: ABC Company, Inc. | | | | FYE Ended: | | |
| Company Fiscal Year Ended: | 12/31/19 | | | 2022 | 2023 | 2024 |
| Date of Transaction Analysis: | 9/25/19 | | Summary of Equity Sponsor Returns | | | |
| Date of Transaction Offer: | 12/31/19 | | Trailing EBITDA Multiple | | | |
| Pro Forma Year: | 2019 | | 5.0x | 25.9% | 26.0% | 25.7% |
| | | | 6.0x | 35.7% | 32.7% | 30.6% |
| Sources of Funds | Amount | %Sources | 7.0x | 44.3% | 38.5% | 34.9% |
| New Equity Sponsor | 5,000 | 40.1% | | | | |
| Rollover | 1,250 | 10.0% | Summary of Mezzanine Holder Returns | | | |
| New Mezzanine w/ Warrants | 1,035 | 8.3% | Trailing EBITDA Multiple | | | |
| New Senior Notes | 2,070 | 16.6% | 5.0x | 21.4% | 19.3% | 18.2% |
| New Revolving Credit Facility | 3,105 | 24.9% | 6.0x | 24.8% | 22.0% | 20.3% |
| Total Sources | $12,460 | 100.0% | 7.0x | 28.1% | 24.4% | 22.3% |
| | | | | | | |
| Uses of Funds | Amount | %Uses | Credit Statistics | | | |
| Proceeds to Seller | 12,764 | 102.4% | EBITDA/Tot. Int. Exp. | | 4.6x | 5.3x |
| Rollover | 1,250 | 10.0% | EBITDA-Capex/ Tot. Int. Exp. | | 3.6x | 4.2x |
| Balance Sheet Cash | (1,554) | (12.5%) | Total Debt/EBITDA | | 3.2x | 2.8x |
| Total Uses | $12,460 | 100.0% | | | | |

# CHAPTER 4

## The Institutional Money Deal™ Process

Once you've built an institutional investment-quality business, you're ready to undertake the IMD process. The first thing to understand about doing an institutional money deal is that it typically takes a minimum of six to nine months. Most IMD-ready businesses hire financial advisors or investment bankers to help represent them in their pursuit of an IMD transaction.

Yes, you can go it alone and perhaps achieve a favorable result, but keep in mind that not knowing what you're doing in this area can be costly in terms of time, effort, and real money. Worse still, business owners attempting direct negotiations can find themselves losing out on significant potential and deserved value—often without realizing it in the midst of complex jargon, structuring, and a buyer's charisma. A good advisor can pay for themselves many times over.

### Sale Process Timeline

Below is a sales process timeline by phase and a list of the specific steps involved. The three phases are (1) preparing to market, (2) marketing, and (3) due diligence and closing.

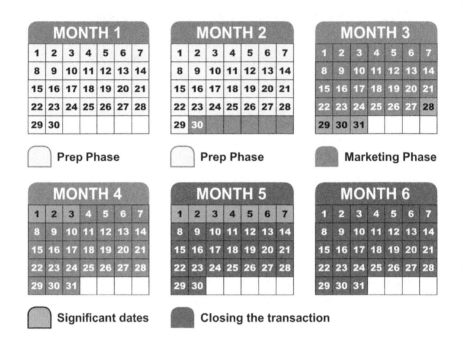

## Sale Process Phase I: Preparing to Market

The first phase of the sale process is the preparing to market phase. During this phase due diligence information is compiled and organized, the confidential information memorandum ("CIM") is written and the list of potential buyers is developed. Below is a step by step description of this phase.

- Weeks 1 and 2: Due diligence information is collected and organized.

- Week 6: Draft of Confidential Information Memorandum completed and reviewed.

- Week 7: List of potential buyers or investors in compiled.

- Week 8: Summary Fact Sheet and Confidentiality Agreement completed. All marketing materials are approved.

## Sale Process Phase II: Marketing the Company

Phase II is the marketing the company phase. During this phase, prospective buyer or investors are contacted, CIMs are distributed, indications of interest are collected, and management presentations are conducted. Below is a step by step description of this phase.

- Week 9: Prospective buyers are contacted.

- Week 11: Data room assembly begins

- Week 12: Management presentation drafted

- Week 13: Dry run of presentation conducted

- Week 14: Potential investors submit initial indication of interest

- Weeks 15 and 16: Potential investors visit the Company are provided access to an online data room.

- Week 18: Final offers received and evaluated, and strategy is determined for moving forward with the final party(ies).

## Sale Process Phase III: Closing the Transaction

Phase III is the closing the transaction phase. During this phase, a letter of intent is negotiated and executed, due diligence is performed, and a purchase agreement is negotiated and executed. Below is a step by step description of this phase.

- Week 19: LOI(s) negotiated with selected party(ies)
- Week 20: Investor(s) due diligence begins.
- Targeted closing is generally 60 to 90 days from signed agreement.

## Confidential Information Memorandum

For starters, IMD folks want to review orderly and professional documents that describe your business in detail and highlight key financial figures. So you need to prepare a "Confidential Information Memorandum," which is a 25-to-50-page marketing document that provides the following information:

1. A list of the company's key investment highlights. This is a description of the top five or six rationales for investing in or buying the business;

2. A description of the company's growth strategy;

3. A discussion of the company's history and key development milestones;

4. A description of products and/or services, including sales and gross margin by product/service;

5. A list of the company's 10 to 20 largest customers by sales volume and gross profit;

6. A description of sales and marketing efforts;

7. An organizational chart and biographies of the management team;

8. A description of all patents, trademarks, and other intellectual property;

9. A description of the company's facilities, lease terms, equipment, and other fixed assets;

10. An overview of the industry and key trends;

11. A list of key competitors and analysis of competitive differentiators; and

12. An income statement, balance sheet, and statement of cash flows for the last three to five years.

## Buyers List

Along with the CIM, you'll need to develop a list of potential institutional investors to contact. Lists of institutional investors can be found in databases like Capital IQ, Preqin, and Pitchbook. There are two types of institutional buyers, financial and strategic. Financial buyers are non-industry buyers who don't typically get too involved in the day-to-day operations of the business. Private equity firms and family offices are examples of financial buyers. These firms are usually staffed by traditional finance people who have little to no direct operating experience.

Strategic buyers are a type of acquirer who is in the same industry as the target company. Unlike a financial buyer, a strategic buyer looks for businesses that can be quickly integrated with its main operations. These buyers do get involved in the operations of the business and may move the business into one of their existing facilities and eliminate redundant general and administrative resources.

## Buyer Criteria

It is important to review each institutional investor's investment criteria to make sure your business is a good fit. For example, the following is the investment criteria of a private equity firm taken directly from its website. When I'm representing a client business, I make sure that the business meets all the relevant criteria.

### Company Characteristics:

- Companies with three-plus years of operating history
- Moderate to strong growth
- Revenues of $5 to $50 million
- EBITDA of at least $1 million
- Experienced management teams
- U.S. based

### Diversified Industries Include:

- Business Services
- Education
- Healthcare
- Manufacturing
- Consumer Products and Services
- Waste and Recycling
- Later Stage Technology
- Distribution

### Investment Size and Structure:

- $3 to $8 million target investment

- Willingness to co-invest with partners
- Control and minority transactions
- Flexible capital structure: subordinated debt and preferred equity

**Transaction Types:**
- Growth Capital
- Acquisition Financing
- Shareholder Liquidity
- Recapitalizations
- Management Buyouts

## Initial Buyer Contact, Teaser, and NDA

If the criteria check out, I'll email them a message like this:

---

**Subject:** Metal finishing services business seeks to be acquired

Joe, we're working with a New England-based metal finishing services business that is seeking to be acquired. Project Allstar is a provider of advanced plating and electropolishing services for aerospace, optical, telecommunications, medical, and electronics customers. Below is a financial summary for the business.

| | 2014 | 2015 | 2016 | 2017E |
|---|---|---|---|---|
| **Sales** | $6.5 | $6.7 | $7.1 | $7.3 |
| % growth | n/a | 3.2% | 6.6% | 1.7% |
| GP % | 41.2% | 44.9% | 42.2% | 42.2% |
| **EBITDA** | $1.3 | $1.7 | $2.0 | $2.0 |
| EBITDA% | 20.1% | 25.0% | 28.6% | 27.9% |

($ in millions)

Please see teaser attached. If you'd like additional information, please execute the attached NDA or feel free to call me with questions.

---

Notice how I referenced a non-disclosure agreement and something called a "teaser." A teaser is a one-to-three-page blind description of a business that is written in "salesy" language and highlights the company's strengths and key features.

## Questions Buyers Will Ask

If the investor group signs the NDA, I'll send them the Confidential Information Memorandum. The potential buyer may have additional questions, so I'll schedule a call to discuss the business and seller's situation in more detail. Questions that buyers typically ask at this point might include the following:

- Why does the owner want to sell?

- Is the seller willing to roll a portion of their equity into a new deal? In most cases, private equity investors want the seller to retain a minority stake (usually in the 20 percent to 30 percent range) in the business for risk mitigation purposes.

- Will the seller and/or management team stay on with the business post-transaction, and if so, for how long? In most cases, investors expect a transition period post-closing to ensure the business doesn't experience any significant interruptions or problems. This transition period could be quite short (days or weeks) in the case of a strategic buyer or several years in the case of financial buyers.

- What is the value expectation of the seller? You almost never want to answer this question directly. Typically, the best answer is, "The market will decide the value," because the optimal approach is to run a process that collects bids from potential buyers rather than having an "asking price." This is because whatever price you say instantly becomes the price ceiling; if you're asking price is too high, buyers won't even participate in the sale process. There is very little upside to giving a specific number.

- What's the process? Are you talking to both financial and strategic buyers? Here the buyer is basically trying to figure out whether or not you know what you're doing and how competitive the process might be, so you need to be careful about what you say. Typically, I'll say that we're talking to several buyers and are expecting indications of interest (IOIs) by a specific date and management presentations shortly thereafter.

## Indications of Interest

The CIM should contain enough information for the potential buyer to make a preliminary bid for the business – the IOI, is basically a letter from a potential buyer or investor that introduces them to the company, indicates a proposed purchase price, identifies sources of financing, a due diligence process, and timing to close. It is important to understand that the IOI is non-binding and terms may change later. A sample indication of interest can be found in appendix B of this book.

Below is a summary of the terms indicated from 10 potential buyers from a process I ran recently. In this case, we received 10 IOIs with valuations for the company ranging from $15 million to $25.4 million. Note that the cash component of the consideration ranged from $10 million to $20.7 million. The balance of proposed consideration consisted of either a seller note or an earnout.

## Cash is King

Cash is king when it comes to sale consideration. I don't think I've ever had a client that didn't understand this concept with complete clarity so no need to belabor the point here.

## Seller Notes and Earnouts

Beyond cash, there are other forms of sale consideration that are often used. The most common are seller notes and earnouts. A seller note is basically an unsecured loan to the buyer of the business to help finance the purchase price. This means you are acting as the buyer's bank. An earnout is an agreement to pay the seller a portion of the company's profits over a specified period after the closing based on a preset formula. For example, a buyer might agree to pay the seller 50 percent of the company's earnings for the two years following the purchase. Earnouts are typically used to bridge valuation gaps between sellers and buyers.

| Firm | Valuation | Cash | Other Consideration | Rollover |
|---|---|---|---|---|
| Buyer #1 | $23.4-24.4m | $19.9-20.7m | n/a | 15% |
| Buyer #2 | $20.0m | $13.5m | $3.5m earnout (50% note) | 15% |
| Buyer #3 | $18.0-$21.5m | $12.6-$17.2m | n/a | 20-30% |
| Buyer #4 | $17.0m | $10.7m | $5.6m in 4-yr. earnout | 20% |
| Buyer #5 | $21.5m | $10.0m | $1.5m note + $2.5m earnout + 10% options | 25% |
| Buyer #6 | $15.0-20.0m | $15.0-20.0m | n/a | 0% |
| Buyer #7 | $21.5-25.4m | $15.0-17.8m | n/a | 30% of post-tax proceeds |
| Buyer #8 | $24.0m | $20.5m | n/a | 15% |
| Buyer #9 | $20.2-22.4m | $15.7-18.9m | $1.5-1.8m seller note | $2.0-2.5m |
| Buyer #10 | $24.0m | $20.0m | 5% of purchase price in seller note | 15% |

## Management Presentations

When I run an IMD process for a client, I like to invite the top five or six bidders to meet with the company and tour its facility. This meeting is called a "management presentation" wherein potential buyers have an opportunity to meet the company's management team and ask questions directly. These meetings typically last two to three hours and feature a PowerPoint presentation of the key aspects of the company's history, strengths, growth opportunities, products and services, customers, leadership and employees, facilities, and financial statements.

## Letter of Intent

After management presentations, I'll ask potential buyers to submit a letter of intent (LOI) by a certain date. An LOI is a binding agreement that lays out the general terms of the investment in the company. At the same time, I'll open an online "data room" that allows potential bidders to review key business documents before submitting an LOI. These documents usually include tax returns, article of incorporation, board minutes, customer data, and product data.

## A Sale Process by the Numbers

Below is a chart showing a sale process step-by-step from the number of buyers contacted to the number of letter intents received in a process we ran relatively recently. As you can, we started off by contacting over 500 potential buyers. Of those buyers contacted nearly 100 returned non-disclosure agreements and received confidential information memorandums. From the

98 potential buyers that received the CIM, 14 sent indications of interest. Of the 14 indications of interest received, we invited six to participate in management presentations. Of the six groups that did management presentations, two issued a letter of intent. We picked on the those letters and intent and eventually closed a transaction with that buyer.

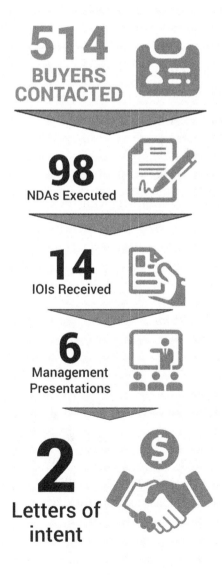

## Due Diligence

After an LOI is selected, negotiated, and signed, the due diligence period begins. This can last anywhere from 30 to 90 days or more. During this period, the buyer investigates in excruciating detail all financial, legal, operational, and industry matters to validate and confirm that the business and its prospects are what it has represented. For example, the investor will likely require any one or all of the following before closing the transaction:

1. A financial audit or quality of earnings report.

2. Legal diligence of corporate filings, loans, contracts, litigation, and regulatory matters.

3. Customer verification calls.

4. Environmental phase one.

5. Background checks of management team members.

6. Employment contracts with key employees and management team members.

Sellers unfamiliar with the due diligence process can become frustrated during this phase of the transaction due to the quantity of information requested, time and resources required to produce documentation, and the overall intrusiveness associated with detailed interrogatories.

## Purchase Agreement and Closing

Also during this period, the purchase and sale agreement is negotiated and finalized. The purchase and sale agreement lays out all the terms of the investment, including representations and warranties of the assets, liabilities, regulatory compliance, and legal matters on the part of the selling shareholders.

A key component of the purchase and sale agreement is the net working capital target. Businesses are usually sold on a debt-free, cash-free basis. Net working capital is the difference between the company's non-cash current assets and non-debt current liabilities. The target is meant to protect both the buyer and seller against significant changes in the company's current assets and liabilities that don't result from fundamental business issues.

For example, if the seller ran up the company's payables and liquidated inventory and accounts receivable during the due diligence period, the buyer would be in a relatively worse position. Likewise, if the company experienced significant sales increases and accounts receivable grew significantly, the seller wouldn't get the benefit of this increase. As a result, a working capital target based on a trailing six to twelve month average is typically used to overcome these types of issues. Any difference between the company's working capital calculation at closing and this target is resolved with a cash credit or debit at closing.

The seller's attorney reviews and helps negotiate the relevant terms associated with this agreement. Typically, there is an escrow of 10 percent or more of the total purchase price that is set aside for potential claims that might arise over the relevant two-to-three-year period after the close. Once the Purchase and Sale Agreement is signed and the relevant funds are deposited via wire transfer, the transaction is closed, and a celebration is in order.

# CHAPTER 5

# The 19 Biggest Mistakes
## That Keep Business Owners from Maximizing Their Multiple

In order to maximize your multiple, you need to avoid some of the more common mistakes business owners make. Of course, there are endless ways to destroy or fail to build value in a business. Those listed below are often hidden obstacles—not front and center on a day to day basis for business owners, but lurking nonetheless in ways that erode value. In some cases, the price of missteps in these categories does not impose itself fully until the end game that is the exit process. Often, the price comes in a form that is firmly quantifiable; that is, value subtracted from the target multiple.

Awareness of these common mistakes can help any business owner avert pain down the road. Here is the list:

1. Not building a big enough company
2. Having significant customer concentration or major customer issues
3. Not running an organized sale process

4. Not going to a broad and large universe of potential buyers

5. Not fully committing to the sale process

6. Not hiring an experienced and competent M&A attorney

7. Waiting too long or getting the timing wrong

8. Not being in touch with the value of your company

9. Losing sight of growth

10. Not focusing on the numbers

11. Not hiring the right team

12. Having poor documentation and processes

13. Not having a succession plan

14. Lacking integrity or character

15. Taking an unreasonable negotiation position

16. Not trusting or accepting the advice of your financial advisor

17. Not accepting market feedback

18. Having a closed mind towards certain buyers or investors

19. Not dealing with significant legal, environmental, or compliance issues

## 1. Not building a big enough company

As discussed previously, failure to build a business of IMD-qualifying scale is the most significant problem entrepreneurs face when they are looking to raise capital or pursue an exit. This point simply cannot be emphasized enough. Institutional investors and corporate buyers have strict criteria for the businesses they invest in or acquire. You can argue that this is shortsighted or foolish on their part. But, recognize that you are swimming upstream if you fail to account for how institutional investors perceive and understand the investment landscape. And if your objective is to do an institutional capital deal, you are playing in their world and under their rules.

I've met many business owners who spent decades building a business only to realize, rather late in the game, that their company had little to no market value. Their only real options at that point were to essentially sell the business for a meager sum or close it entirely.

## 2. Having significant customer concentration or major customer issues

As we discussed previously, customer concentration can be a major issue in a deal. I've had a number of clients that had significant customer concentration issues and been privileged enough to work past them in many instances. However, I once had a client whose primary customer accounted for over 50 percent of total sales. Unfortunately, this client stopped getting orders from this customer just as we got started on a sale process. The situation dealt a heavy blow to the company and its market value. Prospective buyers that had indicated an early interest quickly pivoted away. We put the process on ice as a matter of necessity as the business regrouped and rebuilt its customer base from a hobbled position. Had management taken care years prior to avoid customer concentration, the loss of one customer at this critical interval would have taken a lighter toll.

These are experiences you can only learn from, and move on. When a customer becomes too big a part of your business, you begin to cede control over your destiny and become susceptible to their whims and dictates. At the same time—and what most business owners don't realize is—customer concentration generates a red flag for potential buyers and investors. This is why you should never lose sight of the objective of having a diversified customer base.

### 3. Not running an organized sale process and not using an investment banker

Not running an organized sale process can be costly and time consuming in many different ways. An organized sale process allows you to collect all buyer bids and feedback at the same time so you can easily compare and contrast them. This makes it easier to decide which suitors are most compatible with your goals and objectives.

As mentioned earlier, an investment banker or broker can be instrumental in making sure your sale process is optimized to connect with the best potential partners for your business. This is key to maximizing your multiple. In addition, and importantly, an investment banker provides a buffer between the buyer and seller which can help to minimize the inevitable friction that arises late in the process when significant terms of the purchase agreement are negotiated.

### 4. Waiting too long or getting the timing wrong

Getting the timing of a transaction wrong is one of the most common challenges I've seen. I've worked with business owners who had built great business that had demonstrated years of strong growth and profitability. In more than one instance, I've seen business owners wait too long to sell, starting their sale process only after serious problems began to surface in the business, or after profitability had peaked. A company in decline is one that falls short of maximing its multiple.

I once worked with a manufacturer of automotive accessories that had established a multi-year trend of revenue and profit growth and had just made record sales to a leading big box retailer in their category. Regrettably, not long after trying to sell the business, the company got hit with massive product returns from the same retailer. In retrospect, this situation was foreseeable. The returns from this single customer immediately hit its bottom line and turned an immensely successful and profitable company into a "radioactive" nightmare almost overnight. Buyers who previously exhibited significant interest in the business dropped any pretense of favor immediately upon learning this.

Needless to say, the value of the company fell significantly in a short period of time. This kind of scenario can arise most easily when a business owner loses sight of the risks inherent in the business. No matter how much success you achieve, maintaining a certain amount of caution and concern is healthy; as we all know, you can never eliminate all of the risks in any business. A yearly valuation can help to bring these risks and their remedies to light.

## 5. Not going to a large universe of potential buyers

Many business owners believe they know exactly whom the

perfect buyer for their company is. However, approximately 80 percent of deals are closed with a buyer that the seller did not know previously. In your sale process, the more potential buyers you contact, the more potential bids can be generated. A higher number of bids translates to a higher potential sale price.

In the not-too-distant past, investment bankers might have typically contacted 50 to 100 buyers in a sale process. This target number was the norm for many years, primarily because the process of calling and mailing hard copies of marketing materials was time consuming and costly. However, in today's digital age—coinciding with the proliferation of private equity firms—contacting hundreds and even thousands of potential buyers has never been easier. At my firm, we typically contact 500 buyers or more in a sale process in order to generate at least 10 to 20 initial bids. This gives our clients the best chance of getting a deal done on the most favorable terms possible. This also facilitates the finding of so-called "outlier buyers" who might pay a significantly higher price than anyone else. Of course, potential buyers don't like the idea of competing with hundreds of other buyers, but most accept this as the reality of dealmaking in the modern era.

## 6. Not fully committing to the sale process

A successful sale process requires commitment to see it through. A dip-one-toe-in, "let's give it a try" approach typically isn't productive. Worse still, a non-committed seller can poison the well for future attempts at an exit.

The sale process requires significant time and effort, and a certain degree of difficulty or challenge should be expected no matter how much you might prepare beforehand. Sellers who aren't committed to the process usually don't get the best results because they aren't fully invested in the success of the effort. In most cases, they will bow out of the process when the going gets tough because they have a hard time tolerating any difficulty or challenge. When this happens, the seller will lose credibility; potential buyers will be wary about engaging them in discussions in the future.

## 7. Not selecting an experienced M&A attorney

Hiring an experienced and competent merger and acquisition attorney to handle your deal at the latter stages of the process, alongside your investment banker, is very important. Be careful about using an attorney who doesn't have any transaction experience.

Your long-time corporate counsel could fall into this category. I've seen some in-house attorneys attempt, out of self-interest, to discourage business owners from selling the company. In these cases, where the attorney who has worked for the business in the past is not equipped to represent the company in the transaction, he or she sees a loss of business going forward and can sometimes advise at cross-purposes to the seller.

M&A attorneys are heavily involved at the end of the transaction process when the purchase and sale agreement is negotiated. An under-skilled attorney often doesn't know what to look for at this critical stage. Any misses on the attorney's part could significantly delay the sale and potentially kill the deal altogether. Don't let this happen to you.

Below is a list of questions to pose to a prospective M&A attorney:

- How many transactions have you been involved in?

- Did you represent the buyer or the seller?

- What is the typical size of those transactions?

- How many were unsuccessful? Why?

- What is the cost of your service?

## 8. Not being in touch with the value of the company

As a business owner, knowing your business must include knowing the *value* of your business. I have met many founders who understand with perfect clarity their products, employees, customers, and business models. Surprisingly, these same business owners often could not cite the market value of their companies with any level of confidence. Indeed, it is a rare business owner who has a good sense of what his or her business is worth. In fact, I estimate that less than 10 percent of business owners have ever had a formal valuation of their business done. This is surprising when you consider that most business owners' net worth is tied up in the value of their company.

Where a business owner is not seeking out regular valuations as a strategic imperative, a cascade of missteps can follow. Overestimation of the company's value is one of those missteps. I've met with very successful, competent business owners whose companies were legitimately worth $60 million to $70 million, but who believed (without corroborating data) that they were worth $100 million. Big round numbers can have quite a ring to them, but will not pass muster in a sale process.

One successful executive I met believed his business was worth $30 million. His rationale: one million dollars for every year he'd been in business. These kinds of guessing games, or perhaps wishful thinking, are far more common than you might think.

When I encounter these business owners, I'm candid about what value the market will likely pay for their business versus what is unlikely. And I'm happy to try to get them the absolute best deal I can do for them. But, at the same time, I recognize that I'm not a miracle worker. There is a science to valuation. Eighty to ninety percent of the time, the preliminary valuations I provide are right on the money. If we're off by a significant amount, it's usually because some unforeseen or unspoken issue, whether favorable or unfavorable, creeps up during the sale process.

To emphasize further: As a best practice, I always recommend that business owners have regular valuations of their businesses done. Anyone serious about increasing the value of their business over time should have it evaluated. When performance is measured, it tends to improve.

## 9. Losing sight of growth

Losing sight of the company's growth opportunities is a problem that tends to sneak up on businesses. This is usually because they've achieved a certain degree of success and the owner has already realized the lifestyle he or she desires. Recently, I carried out a deal for a company whose owner was nearly 80 years old and semi-retired from the business. The management team he had in place were solid operators. Most had been part of the business for more than 20 years. Well-compensated and comfortable, they, too, lacked the motivation to continue to keep the business on a growth trajectory. The company had sat on a plateau for quite some time.

So, when we took them to market, buyers saw a great business with a strong and diverse customer base, and great profitability, but one that really hadn't grown much in the previous 4 to 5 years. During management presentations with potential buyers, the President and CFO stated flatly that they didn't know how to grow the business. Growth had not been a priority for them. This was one of those face-palm moments for their investment banker, knowing the true cost of statements like these. The record of poor growth, combined with shoulder-shrugging suggestions of no-growth potential from the management team, dialed back their best offer by millions of dollars. Even simple actions taken along the way to demonstrate a commitment to growth could have kept the business owner closer to securing a maximum multiple.

## 10.  Not having a strong management team in place

The previous example also points to the issue of having the right team in place. Running a thriving and successful business requires that you do at least several things well as a company. You need to have team members who thrive on challenge and do whatever it takes to be successful. Hiring people who have an attitude of entitlement and who take advantage of their position to the detriment of the company and owner aren't people you can afford to keep around.

In the previous example, the managers were paying themselves exorbitant bonuses, buying themselves expensive company cars, and had put their family members on the company's payroll to collect cash without creating value. Because the business owner was semi-retired, he was not fully aware of these actions. They all surfaced during the due diligence process in ways that caught him off guard and diminished the ultimate valuation.

Along these lines, know that buyers will typically perform detailed background checks on all of the company's key executives. In one transaction I was close to, a CFO had to be let go during the process because a background check revealed that he had been involved in financial fraud in the past. Of course, it is better for you and your company if you're able to resolve these types of issues before you undertake a major transaction of this type.

---

## 11.  Not having a handle on the financials

Not having a handle on the company's financials can be a significant problem for any business. I once had a client who had his wife handle all of the company's bookkeeping. Unfortunately, she was a Quickbooks novice without any meaningful bookkeeping experience. The company was a rapidly growing $30 million consumer electronics business with a complicated supply chain and manufacturing processes and approximately 100 employees.

Needless to say that things didn't end well for this company when it undertook a fund raising process to secure growth capital for its rapidly expanding operations. The bulk of its travails could be traced directly to the bookkeeping situation. Efforts to sort through financial records revealed a worst-case scenario: The company had severe cash shortfalls, and there were significant excess production costs and inventory issues that had not been properly accounted for. It didn't help that the founders were very lifestyle focused, making sure to get their action sports vacations, even during critical times in the company's development—A Big Mistake unto itself.

When a qualified accounting professional was finally brought in to bring order to chaos, the company's $5 million profit turned into millions of dollars in losses. The founders had assumed the company to be healthy and high-flying. Suddenly, it was a desperate, distressed firm on the verge of bankruptcy. All of this made conversations with investors very challenging. Eventually, the company was able to secure the funding it needed to continue operations, but only at a severe cost to its shareholders. Concurrently, the company fell behind its lower-quality competitors, who rushed in to fill the void in an industry segment that this company's founders had pioneered. Today, the company is only a shell of the potential and hope it once held.

## 12. Poor documentation and processes

Poor documentation of processes can be absolutely crippling for a business. The companies I've worked with that have excellent, detailed documentation of standard operating procedures, financial reporting, and key reporting metrics have experienced the smoothest paths to a maximum multiple.

On the other hand, I've had clients who took weeks and months to produce simple financial and customer reports, and other documentation. These companies tended to have other problems as well, among them poor profitability, management, financial controls, customer relationships, quality, and employee turnover.

While most peoples' eyes glaze over at the thought of documentation and processes, investors take cues from their strength and quality. How you do anything is how you do everything. Like it or not, mundane documentation and processes are what comprise most of the operations of your business and man-hours from an overall percentage standpoint. So, getting these things done correctly and efficiently is absolutely critical to the overall success of your business, and the success of an ultimate exit transaction.

The company with the best documentation and processes I've ever seen was a logistics business with an exceptionally talented management team, including a highly skilled CFO. The company was able to produce detailed reports almost instantly. Once, when we had a meeting in the company's conference room, the CEO had in hand detailed instructions for operating the audio/visual equipment. Every process was documented, and every document conformed to a process. We assembled the company's data room in a few short days despite the large size of its contents; thousands of pages of company documents were included. It was one of the few transactions I've worked on where we, on the seller side, were actually well ahead of the buyer in fulfilling information requests. The buyer was astounded by the company's ability to deliver timely and relevant information. The strength of the company's performance during the sales process—built from years of excellence in processes and documentation—contributed to the maximization of its multiple at close.

## 13. Not having a succession plan

I'm always amazed when I encounter highly successful business owners working well into their late 60s and 70s. Often, when confronted with questions about succession, ownership transition, or sale, they dismiss the ideas instinctively. Retirement does not interest them. As much as we all stave off thoughts of our own mortality, succession planning is a crucial exercise for any business.

I've met some founders who hold out hope that one of their children will take over their business one day. Often enough, a chosen child is reluctant. Moreover, second-generation business owners rarely fare as well or better than the first. In addition, inter-family fights over business economics and related disagreements are common. And there's nothing quite like a divorce to throw a wrench into even the best laid plans.

You can certainly plan to make your last day of work the day you are carried out in a pine box. But it's important to put some pieces in place so that any end point, expected or unexpected, doesn't precipitate a train wreck for your business. Identifying talent that can take over some of your responsibilities, buying life insurance to cover the relevant estate taxes, and having a plan to transfer economic ownership are all great things to do in advance. Figuring them out at an advanced age, or in a state of less-than-perfect health, is much more difficult.

No matter what your life stage as a business owner, know that thoughtful succession plans serve as an important signal to investors and buyers that your business is poised for a smooth transition at the point at which you are ready for a next chapter.

## 14.  Lacking integrity or character

Most business owners are generally honest people. Most of the time, they do what they say they are going to do and try not to mislead people or misrepresent themselves or their businesses. However, every once in a while, you might encounter someone with no qualms about lying, cheating, or stealing if they believe they can get away with it.

A colleague of mine was once involved in a transaction that

involved someone like this. This integrity-challenged individual was the founder and CEO of a very successful consumer products company that had a great brand name and a significant track record of success. Unfortunately, during the sale of his business, he chose to falsify his customer orders and financial statements, defrauding the buyer and all other parties. He accomplished this by double shipping orders to his largest customer; when the customer returned these "extra" orders, he had them shipped to a warehouse that was off the company's records in order to conceal the returned orders. Regrettably, no one found out about this until after closing. The founder absconded with millions of dollars of the acquirer's money.

Practices like these are reprehensible. Thankfully, they are rare.

The best you can do to prevent yourself from being taken advantage of by an unscrupulous individual is to do your homework. Don't take shortcuts. Pay attention to those gut feelings that might indicate that you're dealing with a less-than-honest person. These types of people usually cultivate charismatic personalities to put people off their trail of clues.

Most due diligence processes are sufficiently robust to catch misdeeds past and present. In some ways, due diligence is its own kind of judgment day. Business owners that have conducted themselves honorably win the day. Integrity is essential to maximizing your multiple.

## 15. Taking an unreasonable negotiation position

Taking an unreasonable negotiation position tests the patience of the parties involved and creates unnecessary drama that threatens to derail any proposed transaction. A certain amount of posturing is expected, but don't get carried away. I've seen a number of buyers and sellers take unreasonable negotiation positions over the years. Recently, I had a client who, after signing a letter of intent (LOI) to sell his company, demanded that the net working capital adjustment be a certain amount despite the fact that the LOI clearly stated that it had to be set based on a trailing twelve-month average. There was no clear rationale for the client's demand, let alone for the way it was couched in the message ("non-negotiable").

The company's accountant had thrust himself into the process in a seeming attempt to gain some investment banking experience at the expense of the client and the process as a whole. Without any consultation with me or others, he shot off an email to the buyer that read, "The net working capital target must be $500k. This is non-negotiable." All he accomplished with this misguided communication was a display of his own ignorance. This attempt at throwing weight and playing hardball came at the wrong time, carried the wrong message, and put the process in unnecessary peril. I spent hours explaining to my client and his accountant the definition of net working capital, its correct application in this context, and the importance of using the company's historical balance sheet data to support discussion of the topic.

Reasonable negotiation positions, grounded in data and knowledge, can pave the way to a maximum multiple. Negotiation in an IMD-quality sale process does not resemble scenes from a made-for-TV drama. Cooler heads prevail. A focus on preserving your top-priority issues, and a willingness to work through and sometimes give on matters of lower importance to you, will generate the win-win scenario that puts your future—and the future of the business you have sold—in the best possible position for the years ahead.

## 16. Not trusting or accepting the advice of your investment banker

This last example leads me to my next point: It is almost invariably a mistake to ignore the advice of your investment banker. A major challenge for business owners embarking on a sale process is the number and range of opinions that flood in from people close to him or her. A sale process can induce anxiety among non-owners who have benefited from their relationship to the business under the status quo.

I've seen a company's long-time contractors, including accountants and lawyers, undermine a deal in the interest of preserving their fees from annual audits and other recurring services. In these cases, these players leveraged the trust they had with a business owner to steer the owner away from a successful exit. As in the example just mentioned, these players sometimes insert themselves in a sale process in ways that are unhelpful. No matter the strength or duration of the relationship, it is important to be aware that others offering opinions may be doing so from a place of self interest.

The investment banker advising you in an exit process will probably be a newer member of your circle. On deal-related issues, the investment banker will have far more knowledge than people who do not work on transactions on a regular basis. Heeding the advice of others without ample transaction experience can cost you dearly in a sale process.

## 17.  Not accepting market feedback

Refusals to accept market feedback rank among the mistakes I've seen most often in a sale process. The market is reality. When you go to market with your deal, and talk to hundreds of potential buyers or investors, the aggregate of their feedback tells you what your company is worth and how attractive it is to potential partners. Rationalizing that these people just don't get us or fail to understand X, Y, or Z is just self-delusion. Although you may get varying opinions from individuals about your business or deal, there is no substitute to talking to market participants in real time.

I once had a client that we'd spent a lot of time and effort carefully marketing and collecting bids for. The few bids we were able to garner came in at X, but this client suddenly decided that he wanted 2X for his company. This business owner failed to recognize that the market had already told him what his business was worth and denying that reality wasn't productive.

## 18.  Having a closed mind towards certain buyers or investors

Having a closed mind toward certain buyers or investors is a significant mistake because it prematurely limits your options. I once had a client who decided he didn't want to sell his company to a private equity firm because he had read negative press about these firms and their operating model. Of course, this person was within his rights to make that call. Still, I believe the decision was shortsighted. Not all private equity firms are the same; not all press about private equity firms is fair or universally applicable. In most deals I've been involved in over my two decades in the business, private equity accounted for approximately 80 percent of the bids I've garnered. Cutting these groups out altogether can significantly limit your options.

Similarly, cutting out prospective buyers from a particular geography, industry adjacency, or other parameter can limit options and upside.

Not wanting to approach a competitor in the sale process is a common concern among business owners. Indeed, these situations present some degree of risk. The best way to minimize these risks is to approach less significant competitors or financial buyers first. Then, once you have a deal surrounded, you can approach the more sensitive competitors at the very end of the process to see if a deal can be done with them. At the latter stages of the process, the risk of problematic competitor behavior is lower. A sale is often imminent at that point.

## 19. Not dealing with significant legal, environmental, or compliance issues

Not dealing with significant legal, environmental or compliance issues can absolutely kill a deal during due diligence. Not too long ago, I had a client that uses a number of hazardous and toxic chemicals in its manufacturing operation. During due diligence, the buyer performed a phase one environmental study which examined the company's environmental compliance procedures in detail. Although the phase one didn't reveal any issues, the buyer's environmental consultants recommended a phase two environmental study. We scheduled a time for them to come back to the company's facility to drill holes on the inside and outside.

Luckily, nothing significant was found in this phase two review. I breathed a sigh of relief. Banks can have a very difficult time financing deals for environmentally challenged businesses because EPA rules and environmental regulations can create a legal nightmare for facilities deemed to be an EPA superfund site: practically everyone who has ever set foot on the premises can be sued. Fortunately, I've never been involved in a worst-case scenario like this before. I hope never to be in the future. Every business that might have to undergo an environmental assessment as part of due diligence should prepare well in advance to avoid any issues.

One former client was involved in litigation with his State's Department of Labor due to alleged independent contractor violations. The lawsuit went to trial right in the middle of the transaction. When my client emerged victorious from the trial, having beaten one of the state's most formidable bureaucracies, it eliminated one potential problem but simultaneously created another. My client, now on a high from beating a rather powerful state agency in court, felt so emboldened that he took on a sense of invincibility and began to issue unreasonable demands of the buyer in short order. I was able to talk him off the ledge more than once and ultimately helped him close a very favorable transaction.

This example, as with the others, points to the role of emotions in driving many of the mistakes highlighted here. A sale process is fundamentally an emotional one for business owners. A strong investment banking advisor can help to manage this ever-present, but almost never-talked-about, aspect of the sale experience.

# CHAPTER 6

## Build a Scalable Business and Focus on Profitable Growth

In order to maximize your multiple, you need to build a scalable business that is focused on profitable growth. Institutional investors want to see clear signs of scalability—it's a foremost concern, typically a determinant of early interest. There are at least five basic strategies that most scalable businesses use in one form or another. These strategies are as follows:

1. Solve a problem

2. Improve a product or service

3. Model a proven winner

4. Change the vertical or niche

5. Partner or affiliate.

Institutional investors will look for signs that your business has executed against one or more of these strategies.

### Solve a Problem

Solving a problem is the foundation of any business. The

creation of automobiles, refrigerators, in-home plumbing, personal computers, accounting software, and smartphones are all examples of products that were created to solve problems. People spend money to solve problems that have a high enough pain point or emotional need, so make sure your offering solves a problem that people are willing to spend money to solve.

## Improve a Product or Service

Improving a product or service means making an existing offering cheaper, faster, or better in some way. Think about some products or services you recently purchased. Could any of them be improved in any way? When was the last time you saw a great movie, ate a great meal, or received excellent service from a business? If you're honest about it, you would probably say that most products and services you purchase are closer to mediocre than great, right? The last time you purchased a truly great product or service, did you tell someone about it? Did you want more? Of course you did. So, while the world is chock full of mediocre products and services, there is always opportunity for great ones.

## Model a Proven Winner

Most people know who the proven winners in their industry are. So why not just copy what they are doing and get the same results? As Picasso said, "good artists copy, but great artists steal." Don't let your ego get in the way of recognizing a proven winner in your field; keeping your pride intact can be a very expensive endeavor. Modeling a proven winner is usually the easiest and surest way of achieving successes. Look at big winners in business today; BlackRock, Netflix, Wal-Mart, and Amazon. Each of their founders meticulously studied the winners in their respective industries before achieving their own success.

## Change the Niche

Changing the vertical or niche is similar to modeling a proven winner, but instead of targeting the same market or product category, you select a different one. For example, an entrepreneur might look at the success a software company had development an application for dentists and decided to development a similar application for chiropractors.

## Partner or Affiliate

There are great, well-managed businesses out there that are always looking for talented people to partner or affiliate with. For example, Amazon, eBay, and Target offer great affiliate programs. Franchises represent a great opportunity for entrepreneurs who want to buy into a proven system that have high success rates.

## Remember: Scalability Matters

Scalability is one of the most important characteristics of an institutional-caliber business. A scalable business addresses a large or rapidly growing market and doesn't face significant limitations to growth that the right people, capital, or strategy wouldn't solve.

For example, a single-location, owner-operated barber shop in a small town isn't a scalable business because it relies on a single person, serves a limited geography, and is unable to accommodate a large volume of customers. However, Great Clips, a hair salon franchise system with over 4,000 locations across the United States and Canada, is a scalable business. Headquartered in Minneapolis, the franchise had system-wide sales of $1.03 billion in 2013. Every location is open seven days a week, features online check-in, and doesn't require an appointment.

Scalable businesses have standardized systems, processes, and procedures that allow them to grow beyond a single owner-operator. This means that employees are trained to follow systems rather than relying on the business owner to make decisions. This is like "idiot-proofing" the business by making it simple enough for people with even modest education, intelligence, or experience to operate.

## The Five Ways to Grow a Business

Once you have a scalable business model, you should focus on profitable growth. There are five basic ways to profitably grow a business:

1. Winning New Customers
2. Margin Expansion
3. Increasing Share of Wallet
4. Introduction of new products and services
5. Selective acquisitions and green fielding

The chart below illustrates a five-year profit growth plan by each of these categories.

**Five Year Profit Growth Bridge** ($ in millions)

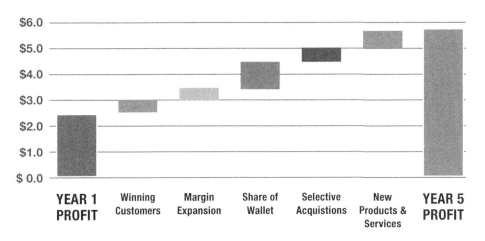

| | | | | | | |
|---|---|---|---|---|---|---|
| **YEAR 1 PROFIT** | **Winning Customers** | **Margin Expansion** | **Share of Wallet** | **Selective Acquistions** | **New Products & Services** | **YEAR 5 PROFIT** |

## Winning New Customers

Winning new customers is about adding customers you haven't done business with previously. Activities that lead to new customer wins include sales, marketing, public relations, and other efforts that lead to interaction with new customer leads. These new potential customers could be within the company's existing market or an entirely new market.

The easiest and quickest way to gain new customers is to work on closing prospects you already have in your pipeline. To accomplish this, think about new ways to approach them to make the sale. Can you make a special limited-time offer? Can someone inside or outside the company call the prospect to find out why they haven't yet done business with you? It often makes sense to offer new potential customers discounts and guarantees to overcome the friction and uncertainty associated with never having done business with you.

## Margin Expansion

Margin expansion efforts involve increasing your price or reducing the cost of delivering products and services to customers. The best way to increase your profit margin is to charge higher prices. If you're in a highly competitive price market, think about ways you can offer additional value to customers and take the focus off your price.

The problem with having the lowest price in your market is that you won't have enough money left over to service customers effectively. You'll have to cut corners to make the math work. This is bad for both you and your customer because you'll be broke and your customer will be unhappy. To increase your prices and move up market to higher quality customers, you might want to consider dropping the bottom 10 to 15 percent of your customer base every year. Highly price-sensitive customers are often the most difficult to serve. I can tell you from personal experience that my most challenging clients have usually been those paying the lowest price. Institutional investors often steer clear of businesses with the lowest margins in their industries.

## The Sales Profitability Formula

The sales profitability formula is as follows:

$$\frac{\text{\# of Sales Opportunities} \times \text{Average Deal Value} \times \text{Win Rate}}{\text{Length of Sales Cycle in Months}}$$

To increase your business's profitability, try increasing any of the items in the numerator—number of sales opportunities, average deal value, or win rate. Otherwise, decrease the denominator (length of sales cycle). Consider the following example: If a company has 10,000 sales opportunities each year, a $1,000 average deal value, a 10-percent average win rate, and a one-month average sales cycle, we'd have the following result:

$$\frac{10,000 \ \times \ 1,000 \ \times \ 10.0\%}{1} = \$1,000,000$$

Now, if the company increased all the numerator items by 10 percent and decreased the sales cycle by 10 percent, do you think sales would increase by 10 percent, 30 percent, or more?

$$\frac{11,000 \ \times \ 1,100 \ \times \ 11.0\%}{0.9} = \$1,478,889$$

As you can see, a 10-percent increase across each dimension leads to a nearly 50-percent increase in profit overall. Even relatively modest improvements can produce significant results.

## Increase Share of Wallet

Increasing share of wallet means selling more to existing

customers or customers that have bought in the past. This could be incremental sales to one of your customers or finding other buyers within the customer's same organization or related organization. Increasing wallet share is a great approach because it's significantly easier to do business with customers you're already doing business with or have done business with in the past. It's more difficult to find completely new customers who don't know you at all. Past and current customers are proven, qualified buyers who've gone through the buying process with you, and you've already validated one another. They obviously liked you and trusted you enough at some point to pull the trigger and purchase your product.

## Introduce New Products and Services

Introducing new products and services involves developing and launching new offerings that can be sold to new or existing customers. These products or services could be for the company's existing market or an entirely new market. While the costs and risks associated with developing and launching new products and services are significant, the benefits can be as well. New product introductions provide businesses the opportunity to set higher prices, earn higher profits, and gain new customers.

## Acquisitions and Greenfielding

Selective acquisitions involve buying other businesses that complement a company's enterprise in some way. These acquisition targets might offer new customers, products, and market opportunities. Greenfielding is the practice of setting up new business locations to service customers in other geographic areas. This is a common approach for retail businesses. Both acquisitions and greenfielding are higher-risk, higher-reward strategies and often require significant capital.

## Investing in Your Business

When I started my first business, I didn't have money to invest in employees, advertising, fancy tools, or equipment. But I did have perhaps the most valuable resource of all, my time and energy. So I focused my time and energy on what I believed to be the most productive activity at the time: winning new customers. I spent several months cold-calling prospective customers trying to find profitable opportunities.

Once I closed my first deal and had some money in the bank, I started investing in advertising and trade show attendance, hired a digital marketing consultant, and purchased software and productivity tools. Basically, I invested a healthy portion of my profits to get in front of more potential customers, provide better service, and increase my efficiency.

Not every spending decision I've made has paid off. I'm constantly trying to evaluate new tools and resources and eliminating products and services that don't prove a significant return on investment. For example, I switched Google Ads consultants at least three times before I found one I thought was great. I tried several online advertising and marketing tools and cancelled them once I saw the ROI wasn't there. Recognize that not every investment will pay off, but don't let that stop you from investing. If you just keep trying, eventually you'll hit pay dirt.

Institutional investors reward companies that have re-invested profits along the way in the interest of building the business and positioning it for further growth.

## Building a Team Around You

Nearly 80 percent of businesses in the United States have no employees and less than $50,000 in annual income. To achieve significant success in business, you need a team of people around you to support you. Forget about doing the solopreneur thing. You can only get so far as a one man band. Hiring a team allows you to leverage your time because employees free you up to focus on the highest value tasks.

To make one million dollars in annual income, you need to make about $500 per hour. Therefore, any activity that can't yield $500 per hour in income should be done by someone other than you. According to the Bureau of Labor Statistics, the average American worker was paid $24.57 per hour in December 2017, or $850 per week. That's about $475 dollars per hour less than what you should be making on an hourly basis, or just 5 percent.

## Leveraging Technology

We live in the golden age of software and technology tools. I don't know why anyone would run a business today without taking full advantage of the many tools available for businesses— tools that allow businesses to automate, streamline, track, and measure virtually every business function, and many of them are relatively inexpensive.

## Advertising

Advertising can be a great way to grow your business and has the potential to achieve returns of 300 to 500 percent on your investment or more. These are much better returns than you'll see in the stock market or practically any other investment you might find. A five-to-one revenue-to-ad-spend ratio is roughly the middle of the bell curve for ad spending. This means that if you spend $100,000 on advertising, you should get about $500,000 in revenue. Good luck making consistent returns like that in any other investment. A ratio over five-to-one is considered strong for most businesses, and a ten-to-one ratio is exceptional. Achieving a ratio higher than ten-to-one ratio is possible, but it shouldn't be expected.

Digital advertising and marketing are a relatively new opportunity for most businesses. This includes Google Ads, Bing Ads, Facebook, LinkedIn, Yelp, and YouTube. Many companies lack any type of digital strategy other than having a website. But these digital platforms offer significant opportunities for business owners who can understand them and be early adopters within their industry or market segment. According to PriceWaterhouseCoopers, the global digital advertising market grew 21 percent to $88 billion in 2017, with Facebook and Google accounting for 90 percent of the growth.

# CHAPTER 7

## Take Inventory of Your Business and Develop a Winning Strategy

nstitutional grade businesses seek to make the most of their resources and opportunities, as well as minimize potential risks and threats. The Strengths, Weaknesses, Opportunities, and Threats (SWOT) framework was designed for this very purpose. A SWOT analysis is most commonly used as part of a marketing plan, but it is also a good tool for general business strategizing. When conducted thoroughly, a SWOT analysis can uncover a wealth of information that can be useful in many situations.

As basic as a SWOT analysis might seem, know that institutional investors will apply the framework to your business as they evaluate it. Your own regular application of the SWOT framework to your business can help to keep you on the road to a maximum multiple.

### SWOT Analysis

A SWOT matrix is usually depicted as a square or rectangle divided into four quadrants. Each quadrant represents one element of the SWOT analysis—Strengths, Weaknesses, Opportunities, Threats. Strengths and weaknesses relate to internal aspects of the business, like high product quality, strong sales and marketing capabilities, and lack of financing. Opportunities and threats are external characteristics of the business's market environment. These might include digital advertising, new distribution channels, and low-cost competition.

| INTERNAL ANALYSIS | EXTERNAL ANALYSIS |
|---|---|
| Strengths | Opportunities |
| Weaknesses | Threats |

To begin filling in each quadrant of the matrix, use the list of questions below. For the Strengths quadrant, think about the attributes of your business that will help you achieve your objectives using the following questions:

- What does your business do well?
- What are your unique skills?
- What expert or specialized knowledge do you have?
- What experience do you have?
- What do you do better than your competitors?
- Where are you most profitable in your business?

For the Weaknesses quadrant, think about the attributes of your business that could hurt your progress in achieving your objectives, and consider the following questions:

- In what areas does your business need to improve?

- What resources do you lack?

- What parts of your business are not very profitable?

- Where do you need further education and/or experience?

- What costs you time and/or money?

For the Opportunities quadrant, think about the external conditions that will help you achieve your objectives:

- What are the business goals you are currently working towards?

- How can you do more for your existing customers or clients?

- How can you use technology to enhance your business?

- Are there new target audiences you potentially can reach?

- Are there related products and services that provide an opportunity for your business?

For the Threats quadrant, think about the external conditions that could damage your business's performance:

- What obstacles do you face?

- What are the strengths of your biggest competitors?

- What are your competitors doing that you're not?

- What's going on in the economy?

- What's going on in the industry?

Below is a completed SWOT matrix I did for one of my clients in the transportation and logistics industry.

| STRENGTHS | WEAKNESSES |
|---|---|
| <ul><li>High profit margin</li><li>Strong track record of growth through mergers and acquisitions</li><li>Strong systems, procedures</li><li>Use of technology</li><li>Premier customer accounts</li></ul> | <ul><li>Significant customer concentration (2 customers make up nearly 50 percent of sales)</li><li>No long-term customer contracts in place</li></ul> |
| OPPORTUNITIES | THREATS |
| <ul><li>Growth via acquisitions</li><li>Geographic expansion through green fielding</li></ul> | <ul><li>Lawsuit with the state Department of Labor</li><li>Competitive market dynamics</li></ul> |

One of the most important parts of your SWOT analysis is using the data you compiled to identify new strategies and goals for your business. For example, you can:

- Create a plan to build up your strengths even more;

- List ways you can work on repairing your weaknesses;

- Set goals for each of the opportunities you identified; and

- Devise a plan to use your strengths to decrease the threats you identified.

Another exercise that can be valuable is looking for ways to combine data from different quadrants in even more ways:

- Explore how you can combine your strengths and opportunities to develop new strategies;
- Try combining strengths and threats to identify threats you can eliminate;
- Look at your weaknesses and opportunities to create a list of areas ready for improvement; and
- Make a list of areas to avoid that fall under weaknesses and threats.

Once you understand how to compile your SWOT data and find ways to use it strategically, the SWOT analysis can be a tool you can use over and over in your business to explore new opportunities and improve your decision-making process.

## Generalist vs. Specialist

The most successful and profitable businesses in most markets avoid positioning themselves as generalists and move up the value hierarchy by becoming specialists to maximize their value in the marketplace. This is somewhat counterintuitive because most business owners want as many customers as they can get, and being a specialist means you're proactively ignoring a significant part of the market. We'll discuss why this is usually a better strategy than being a generalist. But first, let's talk about what a generalist is.

A generalist has no specific target market or specialized product offering. It tries to be all things to all people. Basically, it takes all comers and makes no significant attempt to specialize its product offering or tailor the marketing message to a specific market. This is usually a less-effective approach because you end up with either a weak marketing message or a product offering with limited value to customers, or both. The essence of a successful business is the product-market fit, so think about how to optimize your offering along these parameters.

For example, consider a general contractor who just tries to take any work it can get versus a custom builder focused on high-end, luxury homes in a specific zip code. Which one do you think will have a more consistent, relevant, and differentiated approach to marketing, branding, and sales messaging?

Specialists pick a specific market segment and/or product and focus on it to the best of their abilities. They don't try to be all things to all people. Specialists have an easier time winning business than generalists because most people would prefer to hire a specialist than a generalist. Buyers usually believe specialists understand them and their needs better than generalists. For example, most people would prefer a heart specialist than a general practitioner doctor to perform open-heart surgery.

Not only do specialists win business more easily, but they can charge higher prices than generalists because customers tend to perceive specialists as offering more value. Higher prices mean higher profits, and higher profits means more money to service customers. The perception of better service becomes a reality.

## Positioning as an Authority

Even better than a specialist is an authority.  An authority is recognized within the market as an expert.  Authorities are leaders in their respective market and are often featured in industry publications and events.  Authorities are sought after for their knowledge and ability to solve challenging problems.  Here's a diagram of the value positioning hierarchy.

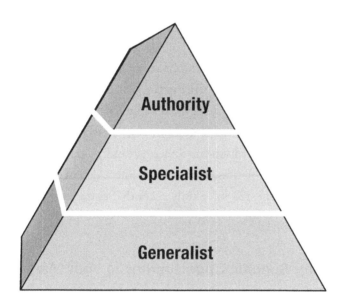

## Where Opportunity Lies

Thomas Edison once said, "Opportunity is missed by most people because it is dressed in overalls and looks like work." An excellent way to identify opportunities in your market is to consider what your competitors are not doing. For example, are your competitors taking full advantage of digital marketing and social media? What about traditional marketing strategies like article publishing, cold calls, and personal visits? Look at the list below and consider whether these present opportunities for your business.

| YouTube | Twitter | Cold Calls |
|---------|---------|------------|
| Facebook | ITV | Emails |
| Instagram | Radio | Personal Visits |
| Snapchat | Articles | Letter |
| LinkedIn | Press Releases | Networking |

If you're wondering if any of these present opportunities for your business, the answer is affirmative, because few businesses, if any, use all these tools at all, let alone all of them effectively. And the fact that business leaders in your market aren't using them doesn't necessarily mean they're stupid. The most likely reason is that many of these media came into existence relatively recently, and businesses have only recently begun using them.

## Identifying Specific Opportunities in Your Market

A great framework for identifying opportunities in your market is blue ocean strategy. In Renée Mauborgne and W. Chan Kim's book <u>Blue Ocean Strategy: How to Create Uncontested Market Space and Make Competition Irrelevant</u>, they propose that businesses can have more success by creating a blue ocean, rather than trying to compete in the red ocean – the traditional market space that is filled with "sharks," also known as fierce competitors. Key insights for developing a Blue Ocean Strategy are as follow:

1.  Don't try to outperform competitors.

2.  Create a new market space to make competitors irrelevant.

3.  Value innovation is the key to creating a blue ocean strategy.

4.  Value innovation simultaneously pursues low cost, and differentiatio

To develop a blue ocean strategy, ask yourself these questions:

- What factors in your industry are taken for granted and can be eliminated?

- Which factors in your industry can be reduced below industry standards?

- Which factors should be raised above industry standards?

- What new factors that have never been offered can be created?

Other key takeaways from the book include:

- The only way to beat the competition is to stop trying to beat the competition.

- To focus on the red ocean is to accept the key constraining factors of the market and competition — limited opportunity and the need to beat a competitor to succeed—and to deny the distinctive strength of innovative businesses. which is the ability to create new and uncontested market space.

- To fundamentally shift the strategy canvas of an industry, you must reorient your strategic focus from competitors to alternatives and from customers to noncustomers.

# CHAPTER 8

## Building Your Top Line

nstitutional investment-grade businesses typically have at least $10 million in annual sales or more. Only a small percentage of businesses, less than 3 percent, achieve sales volume of this magnitude. To get into that group, you're going to need superior sales and marketing skills, a high level of activity, and significant commitment. Initially, you'll need to focus on the top line more than the bottom line, because most companies never get big enough to matter much to anyone, let alone institutional investors.

### 80 Percent of Businesses Do Less Than One Million Dollars in Sales

As you can see from the chart below, less than 20 percent, or fewer than one in five businesses in the United States, have annual sales of one million dollars or more. From there, the percentages drop rapidly. When we look at companies with sales of $10 million or more, we're talking about approximately 2.5 percent of all businesses. That's only one in forty. As you can see, when we're talking about businesses with sales of $10 million or more, we're talking about a very exclusive group.

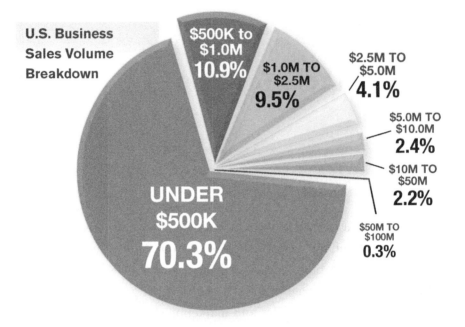

U.S. Business Sales Volume Breakdown

$500K to $1.0M **10.9%**

$1.0M TO $2.5M **9.5%**

$2.5M TO $5.0M **4.1%**

$5.0M TO $10.0M **2.4%**

$10M TO $50M **2.2%**

$50M TO $100M **0.3%**

UNDER $500K **70.3%**

## Focus Primarily on Sales and Marketing

As a business owner, you should spend about 60 percent of your time and money on sales and marketing because this is typically where most incremental value can be created. In most cases, you shouldn't spend more than 40 percent of your time and resources on other business functions like operations and production since these usually don't contribute as much to the long-term value of a business.

Peter Drucker, widely considered to be the founder of modern business management, said, "The purpose of a business is to create a customer." Since this can only be accomplished with sales, I would argue that sales is the single most important

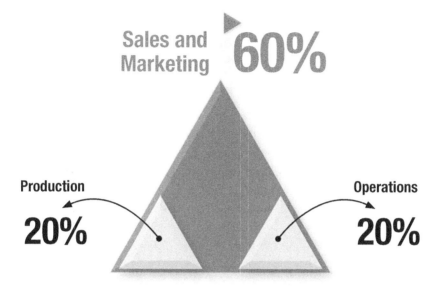

function because you don't have a business without it. I think it is particularly interesting that even leading business schools, for the most part, have ignored sales education. They do a great job on marketing, finance, strategy, operations, management, and virtually every other relevant business functional area, but they fail to teach students selling fundamentals and how to close transactions.

There's a lot of ignorance and more than a few misconceptions about selling that prevent people from achieving sales success. There also are some foundational concepts around selling that, if you fail to understand and appreciate, you'll experience significant frustration, anxiety, and other negative emotions about selling. If you have a complete understanding of sales, you'll understand that sales is a way to serve others, demonstrate leadership, and demonstrate a deep commitment to your goals and purpose in life.

## People Buy to Solve Problems

A key selling fundamental to understand is that people only buy products and services to solve problems. As discussed in the chapter on scaleability, solving a problem is essential for your business. People don't buy a drill to own a drill, for example; they buy a drill because they need to make a hole. Identifying the problem your customer is trying to solve is an important part of the sales process. In fact, selling is a great way to serve others because you are helping them solve problems.

## The Power of Agreement

The first rule of selling is, always agree with the customer. Whenever you are faced with an argumentative, disagreeable, or unreasonable customer, just say, "OK, I understand" or "Yes, I agree" and get back to selling and closing. In many cases the customer is just testing your attitude and sales skills. Getting into an argument with customer is a sure-fire way to upset them and make them not want to do business with you. Don't fall into this trap. Keep your attitude positive and helpful no matter what the customer says.

Even if what the customers say isn't really reasonable, agreement gives you the chance to move them to a more reasonable position later. Some might say faking agreement with someone is lying or deception. But saying you agree could also mean you understand their point of view or perspective and appreciate their thoughts and feelings. Some people just need to feel understood before they can be convinced to do business with you. Maybe they're just looking for a little empathy and understanding in a cruel and difficult world. If you take the time and effort to show some understanding, you will be rewarded.

I once had a prospect with a challenging personality. She had initially contacted me through my website, so I emailed her additional information about my services. I like to call prospects within minutes of initial contact to learn more about them and offer information, but she wouldn't take my direct call and insisted via email that I schedule a time to talk via Skype or FaceTime.

I thought this was a little strange, but I went with it. Unfortunately, when time for our FaceTime call came around, her scheduling software provided no information about how to initiate the call. I emailed her to ask how to proceed, and she replied back, "Are you serious? We'll find someone else to help us…" For a second, I thought this person was clearly unreasonable, and I didn't need this kind of aggravation. But, I quickly came to my senses and replied, "I apologize for the misunderstanding here. When I scheduled the FaceTime meeting, I didn't get instructions about how to initiate it. I can understand your frustration. I'd be happy to speak with you at any time today." She contacted me shortly thereafter and ended up hiring us. It would have been easy for me at any point in the sale process to decide this person was too difficult, but I never would have gotten the sale if I'd given up.

## There's No Such Thing as a Born Salesperson

Salespeople are made, not born. I know a saleswoman with a great, outgoing personality and strong interpersonal skills. If you met this person, you'd think that she is the quintessential salesperson type—outgoing, fun, thoughtful, and considerate, and she truly believes that she is a great salesperson. However,

I can tell you she really struggles with closing sales. "I don't want to be pushy," she says. Her problem is that she sells based on her personality rather than taking a systematic approach to selling and closing. She cares more about keeping her ego intact than ultimately being successful. Also, she fails to understand that selling is only half of the equation. You must know how to close.

If you met me in person, you probably wouldn't think of me as a strong salesperson, but you could put me up against the most naturally charismatic person you can imagine who hasn't been trained, and I'll out sell them many times over. The best thing you can do for your sales team is to get them on a regular sales training program. I recommend Cardone University, an online, on-demand sales training platform you can use anywhere with an Internet connection.

## Rejection

We can't talk about sales with mentioning the "R" word: rejection. Rejection is responsible for the death of more sales careers and entrepreneurs than probably anything else. How many times have you heard someone say, "I can't do sales because I don't like rejection?" Every time I hear this, I think that just living on planet earth is going to be a problem for you. Everyone experiences rejection in life, and to be successful in business, just as in life, you need to get your head straight on this topic.

I think it's safe to say no one likes rejection. If you know someone who does, you might want to help them take stock of that. Rejection is what one experiences when their sales pipeline is too small. Think about a massive sales pipeline, chock full of exciting sales opportunities and prospects. How disappointed would you be if just one prospect didn't buy from you? Probably not much, right?

Rejection is an indication that your sales pipeline is too small and that your business model is broken. The reason you experience disappointment is not because of the obvious sales failure but the unconscious realization that something you're doing is wrong and needs to be fixed. That fix is creating significantly more sales activity.

The fact that the customer says "no" and doesn't buy is not a reason to be upset, unless of course, you don't have any more customers in your pipeline. If the customer says no but there are 10 more people waiting to buy, you may actually be relieved, because you can focus your time and efforts on those willing and able to do business with you.

## Believe in Your Product

Belief in your product is an essential part of selling. To be an effective salesperson, you must believe your product offers significantly more value to the customer than it costs. When you're talking to a lead on the phone or in person, you must believe your product is right for the customer. Conviction is the make-or-break point in sales, because when two people interact, the more certain person's point of view will typically prevail.

I once had an investment banking client for whom I'd secured a lucrative letter of intent from a large private equity firm to purchase his business. We had a 90-day due diligence period to get through before the closing and a lot of work to do in the meantime. However, my client perceived the buyer to be somewhat slow and unresponsive, and he began questioning the buyer's commitment to follow through on the deal. He would call me almost every day and say things like, "There's no way they're going to close..." and "These guys aren't serious buyers..." During these times, I would listen to his concerns and work on productive solutions, but never did I allow him to convince me that the deal wasn't going to happen.

I should note that my client was a 30-year industry veteran who had built his business through nearly 20 acquisitions and had been down the road with private equity buyers in the past, so he was no neophyte when it came to deal making. He was intelligent and accomplished in his own right. The private equity firm was a large and successful fund with more than $3 billion under management and had acquired hundreds of companies. Both parties had large egos, highly disagreeable, ultra-competitive personalities, money driven orientations, and little patience for monkey business. Both groups were complete sharks, and there I was stuck between them trying to make a deal happen.

After 90 days without closing, my client sent the buyer a termination letter, and it appeared he had been right all along. However, that wasn't the time to give up. I worked with both the buyer and seller for several more weeks, overcoming several impasses that threatened to completely derail the transaction until we finally closed the deal. If I had given up, lost belief, or confidence in my ability to help find a pathway forward at any point along the way, this deal would not have happened. I never allowed my client or the buyer to convince me that we couldn't work through our differences. The result was a successful outcome for all parties.

## Follow a Sales Process

Effective selling follows a step-by-step process that moves potential customers through a series of steps. The sales generation cycle starts with getting attention for your offering, identifying leads, and moving those leads through additional steps that result in closing a sale. Below is a chart of the sales generation cycle with detailed explanations of each step.

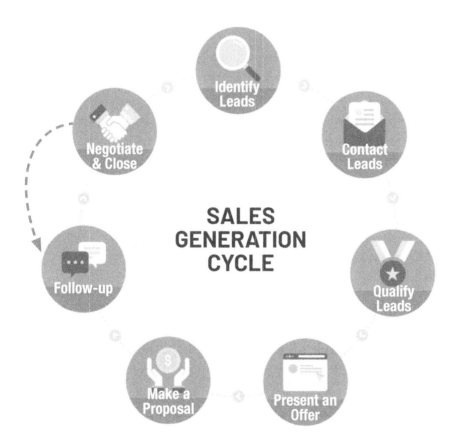

When it comes to sales, the biggest problem most businesses have is obscurity. No one knows who you are or what you do. Let's face it, not many businesses are household names. Everyone knows big companies like Apple, Google, Coca Cola, Nike, Bank of America, and McDonalds. But there are literally millions of businesses you have never heard of, that offer great products and services, and are led by great people. This is because only the largest companies can afford national advertising campaigns.

The fact no one knows your business is a problem because people need to know who you are to buy your products and services. This means you need to get significant attention in your market. The proliferation of new media platforms means that there are now more channels than ever through which to garner attention for your business, no matter how small or large it is. Many of these newer platforms require more time, creativity, and energy than money. Take advantage of them, because the chances are that if you don't, your competitors will.

## Speed Matters

Speed is important in sales success. Once you get a lead, you need to get into communication with that lead as soon as possible. Don't sit on a lead just because you want to seem busy or important or don't want to appear desperate. The average company takes almost seventy-two hours to follow up a lead. This is a ridiculously long period of time. Think about the last time you needed a plumber, auto repair, or dental care. Were you patient enough to sit around for three days for someone to call you back? Research shows that contacting a prospect within the first five to ten minutes increases your chances of getting into communication with them by more than ten times.

The faster you can sell, the faster you can reach your targets and, eventually, the Institutional Money Deal winners circle.

## Qualify the Buyer

Once you contact the lead and answer their questions, work to qualify them as buyers. Here is a list of the key buyer qualifications:

1. Decision maker: Is the person you're talking to able to make a decision to buy? If not, who is that person?

2. Wherewithal: Is the customer financially qualified to buy the product you're offering? If not, you may want to move on and focus on other leads.

3. Sold on the product: Is the customer convinced the product your offering is right for them, or are they still considering other options? If not, go back through your sales process and see if you can identify where you lost them.

4. Belief in you: Does the customer have confidence that you are the right provider? If not, don't be afraid to ask them why they are uncertain about working with you.

5. Urgency: Does the customer feel the need to buy now? If not, try to find out if the reason they aren't ready is just a stall or a "legitimate" reason.

People love options, and you should always provide your buyer with options, even when it appears your buyer is already committed to the product you're offering. Presenting options to customers helps them view you in a more consulting role and allows you to offer a range of products offerings for negotiations rather than cutting your prices.

## Always Make a Proposal

Be sure to make a proposal to every prospect regardless of whether you think they're a "serious" buyer. Many sales are lost because the salesperson just didn't make a proposal to the customer in the first place. This is usually because the salesperson fears rejection. A salesperson may even rationalize not making a proposal because they don't want their closing ratio to be negatively affected. But what do you really have to lose? You've already spent time with the prospect and demonstrated your offering. You might as well just make the proposal and at least have a chance at making a sale. The reality is that you never know whether someone is a buyer until you actually ask and ask again.

## Closing the Sale

Closing involves a very different mindset and process than selling. Once you've gone through your sales process, made a proposal to a decision-maker who is qualified to buy and who's convinced your product is right for them, you've entered the close. Everything you've done for the customer up to this point is of no value to anyone if you don't close the sale, because no value has been created until there's an exchange.

Some salespeople might struggle with this idea and rationalize that their presentation was valuable or they were helpful to the prospective buyer even if they didn't sell anything to them. But the buyer receives no benefit until you both agree to do business together and a product is exchanged for payment. If the buyer offers an excuse for not closing, probe them to see whether it's just a complaint or a valid objection. The only way to know for sure is to press forward with the close.

In the appendix, I've included a list of buyer objections and closing lines to support your team in increasing sales. At the end of the day, the multiple you are awarded at exit is a reflection of your success in selling.

## Follow-Up

If you are unable to close the buyer during the first contact, you'll need to follow-up with them later. Follow-up is the secret to an effective sales process. The reason why follow-up is so powerful is because only about 2 percent of customers buy on the first contact. If you only spoke with a customer once, you'd only close a sale about 2 percent of the time. However, about 80 percent of customers buy after five to twelve contacts. So if all you did was contact your prospects at least five to twelve times, your closing ratio would increase by about 40 times on average.

When you consider that 48 percent of salespeople never do any follow-up whatsoever and that 64 percent of companies admit they don't have an organized way to nurture a lead, a massive opportunity becomes apparent. I was recently in the market for a homebuilder to construct a home on a lot I've owned for several years. I met and interviewed at least six different builders, showed them the lot, and told them what I wanted. However, not even one followed up with me on their own. I was surprised none made much of an effort to win my business, and I had to chase these guys down for quotes and proposals. This experience made me think there might be a significant opportunity to get into the building industry, because it was so obvious to me how broken the sales process was.

There are two important keys to successful follow-up -- organization and creativity. Good follow-up requires organization, excellent systems, and significant commitment. First and foremost, you need a good Customer Relationship Management (CRM) system to keep track of your prospects' contact information and notes. Good follow-up is always creative and uses a variety of ways to stay in front of the prospect. You don't want to simply say "are you ready to do business?" every time you speak with them. You need creative communication that demonstrates interest in them as a customer. Emails, newsletters, calls, texts, personal visits, and handwritten notes should all be part of your regular follow-up repertoire.

# CHAPTER 9
## Mindset

**W**hen I reflect upon the many transactions in which I've participated, a common theme emerges: *a business owner's mindset matters.* I couldn't end this book without commenting on this important reality.

For many business owners, the sale of their business brings a roller coaster of emotions. There is the elation at the sight of first-round bids; and the nervousness that precedes it. There is the impatience and aggravation that can creep in during due diligence. There is the simultaneous joy and sorrow that so many owners experience as a sale is finalized.

To transfer ownership of your life's work into the hands of another carries with it an emotional component—and, often, an emotional toll—that must be acknowledged. Business owners who understand not only the mechanics of a sale process, but also the psychology of it, are best positioned to see a process through to a maximum multiple.

This final chapter tackles that psychology head on, with an outline of reminders on mindset that can make all the difference the sales-process context.

## Stay focused, committed and attentive

The pace of a sales process—and the perception of its pace—tends to vary at different stages. At earlier stages, when the deal first goes to market, business owners will often say something along the lines of, "Whoa, this is going so much faster than I expected it would." This is often an emotional reaction to the idea of a sale becoming a reality. More than a few owners request that the effort be slowed at the go-to-market interval as fear, and sometimes cold feet, start to set in. These feelings can send some owners into backward motion or slow motion, to their detriment in the short- and long-term.

Later, during due diligence, some of these same owners express a sense that a snail's pace has taken hold. Some become disengaged from the details, even to their peril. Deal fatigue presents real dangers. It is often said that time kills all deals. The longer a deal drags on, the more likely it is that the buyer, seller or both will lose patience with the transaction and decide to cut their losses and move on. Don't be the seller who loses patience without cause, or the seller who loses focus, condemning the process to a premature end.

Timelines for successful business sales are well established. Ultimately, every stage requires your full engagement and attention. The maximum-multiple reward goes to owners who participate and perform fully and at their best through the entirety of the effort.

## Stay Self-Aware

Recognize the tides of challenging emotions as they roar toward you in a sales process. Doubt, fear, grief, greed, anger, pride, and many other impulses can grip even the steadiest business owner when a process is underway.

In particular, there is the anxiety factor. As a process marches forward, sellers often experience escalating worry over what will happen to their business, their employees, and customers once it is sold and no longer under their control. These are reasonable concerns. Even so, it's important to bear in mind that when a buyer steps up to pay millions of dollars for a business, they usually have every incentive they need to keep the business intact and running on an even keel.

When millions of dollars are on the table, many people morph into a version of themselves they would not recognize. I have seen people's inner demons surface in these moments, bringing later shame and embarrassment. A good investment banking advisor can help you keep these demons at bay. Even so, know that your worst self—an even darker, more monstrous version than you yourself have ever known—can rage without warning at the negotiation table.

Self awareness at the first onset of destabilizing emotions is critical. It's always useful to remember that the sale of your business is a major life event. Accordingly, emotions will run high. Keeping yourself in check, and keeping the cylinders from falling off, requires you to stay self-aware.

## See the Big Picture

When anxiety, deal fatigue and unproductive emotions loom, it helps to take a step back and appreciate the big picture.

When you participate in the sale of a company, you are realizing the promise of an economic system that rewards entrepreneurial risk-taking, talent and hard work. You are preserving the values upon which it rests—values that propel and sustain the innovations improving lives everywhere, everyday. That, my friends, is the ultimate multiple.

# APPENDIX A

## Sample Indication of Interest

PRIVATE & CONFIDENTIAL

Dear Jon,

Investment Partners is pleased to provide this non-binding indication of interest with respect to the potential acquisition of ABC Company ("ABC" or the "Company"). Based on our review of the confidential information memorandum and our subsequent discussions with you, we believe ABC is an attractive investment opportunity, and we are excited about the prospect of partnering with the management team through the Company's next phase of growth. We are especially impressed by the Company's diversified customer base, experienced leadership team, technical capabilities, and attractive growth opportunities. Based on our experience with many businesses, we believe we will be value-added partners to the management team going forward.

Based on the information that we have gathered to date, we would contemplate an acquisition of the Company assuming a cash-free, debt-free enterprise value of $10 to $12 million. We view the Company's day-to-day management team as a critical ingredient to its success, and our investment thesis relies on their continued leadership going forward.

We anticipate financing the transaction with a combination of third party debt and junior capital from Investment Partners committed fund. Concurrently with closing the transaction, we would propose creating an incentive unit pool to provide the members of the leadership team with equity participation in the business. Based on Investment Partner's committed fund and our strong relationships with many senior lenders, we are confident in our ability to secure the necessary financing required to consummate the transaction. (cont.)

The investment would be subject to business and legal due diligence satisfactory to Investment Partners as well as the completion of legal documentation. We would expect to consummate a transaction within 60 days of executing a letter of intent. The submission of this non-binding indication of interest reflects preliminary approval from Investment Partners to pursue this acquisition with final approval conditional upon the completion of satisfactory business and legal due diligence.

We look forward to discussing our proposal, and the appropriate next steps, with you at your earliest convenience. Thank you again for the opportunity to present our proposal, and do not hesitate to call us with any questions.

Sincerely,
Investment Partners

# APPENDIX B

## Buyer Objections and Closes

### Buyer Objections

All buyer objections fall into one of four categories:

1. Time: The buyer can't buy right now and must wait for some reason.

2. Money: The buyer doesn't have the money and isn't financially qualified to buy.

3. Stall: The buyer is avoiding a decision due to uncertainty or some other reason.

4. Product: The buyer isn't set on the right product and should be offered a different product. This is actually the most common objection and why you should offer multiple products.

To effectively respond in the moment to any objection a buyer might raise, you need to have memorized responses that specifically address any potential issue. Below is a list of 24 of the best closes that can be used for some of the most common situations and objections. I've compiled this list from some of the best authors on the topic of closing sales including Grant Cardone, Brian Tracy, Zig Ziglar and others. This is not meant to be an exhaustive list of closes. If you would like a more comprehensive resource, you should check out *The Closer's Survival Guide*, by Grant Cardone.

Also, these closes are written from the perspective of salesperson selling over the phone rather than in person. If you typically sell face-to-face in a "retail" setting, you will want to modify these closes accordingly.

## General Closes

### Move Forward Close

"Are you ready to move forward? I can send over the contract right now."

### Get Started Close:

"When would you like to get started? Today or later this week?"

### Scale from 1 to 10 Close:

"On a scale of one to ten, how would you rate our proposal? (wait for answer) What would make it a 10? (wait for answer) Great, I'll get that handled for you. Can you sign and return the agreement today?"

### Two Choices Close:

"Taking all of your requirements and desires into consideration, I think these two products would work best for you. Would you like to go with [X] or [Y]?"

### Proposal Changes Close:

"Would there be any changes or additions you would want made to the proposal before we come to an agreement on the pricing?"

### Paperwork Close:

"Whose name will we be doing the paperwork in, your name, the company's name or both?"

**Lock Close:**

"Would there be any reason you would change your mind about this decision?"

---

## Pricing Closes

**Agreement Close:**

"I agree that it's a lot of money and everyone that has bought this product has said exactly the same thing. Can you sign and return the agreement today?"

**Do it Anyway Close:**

"I understand that it's more money than you budgeted, do it anyway."

**No Shortage of Money Close:**

"I agree it's a lot of money, but there is no shortage of money in the world. There is a shortage of people who achieve their goals. Let's do this."

**You Knew That Already Close:**

"I agree it's a lot of money, and I suspect you knew this would be a lot of money before. Will you sign the agreement today?"

**I'm Over Budget Close:**

"Everyone who buys here is over budget, but we all still work it out.

**Price Guarantee Close:**

"Since price is your main concern, I'm going to offer you our price guarantee that we will match any other offer you find."

## Stall and Timing Closes

### Think About it Close:

"Thought is instantaneous. Think about sitting on the beach sipping a margarita. Did you get the picture? You see, thought is immediate. What you need to do now is make a decision. Yes or no. Do or don't do. I'm fine with either one. Which is it?

### Third Party Stall (I Need to Talk to My Partner) Close:

"What if your partner says no? (answer: he won't) Then let's do this." (answer: yes) Will he say no to the money or the product? (get answer and resolve)

### If Everything Were Right Close:

"If everything were right, would you buy our product right now? (answer: Yes) So what is it: the price, the product, the terms, me or my company?"

### Three Reasons Close:

"When people have difficulty making a decision, it's usually for one of three reason: the product, the price, or the company. Which one these is the reason that's holding you up?"

### Think About it Close II:

"I understand. However, you thinking about it will not change the fact that this product serves your objectives and needs, and you are going to do it sooner or later. Let's get this done so that you can think about the other things that require your attention."

### I've Said the Same Thing Close:

"I understand and as a consumer myself I have said the same thing when I (1) didn't want to confront the salesperson; (2) didn't want to disappoint the salesperson; and (3) there was a concern that hadn't been addressed. Which one is it for you?"

### Apology Close:

"I really need to apologize to you for not being able to come to an agreement with you. Can I ask you – was it something I did? Was it something I failed to do? (answer: no) Then let's do this now."

### Scarcity Close:

"As you are aware, we have limited availability for this offering and significant demand. I want to be certain that we can get you what you want; can you sign and return the agreement today?"

### Never the Best Time Close:

"There is never a best time to make this decision as there will always be something going on. Let's get this done so that you can start benefiting now. Can you sign and return the agreement today?"

### Buyer Says, "I'm Going to Wait" Close:

"You can certainly wait if you'd like. Let me just share with you what happens while you wait. (1) you and your company still need the product. (2) It is costing you not to have the product. (3) Nothing changes except the price of doing this in the future may be higher. Let's do this and get it done since you have many other things to put your attention on. Can you sign and return the agreement today?"

### Future Date Close:

"Since I am unable to get you to do this today, can I at least get a commitment and agreement from you to do this with me at some time in the future?"

# ABOUT THE AUTHOR

Jon is the Founder and Managing Partner of Stanton Park Capital (www.stantonparkllc.com), an investment banking firm providing merger and acquisition, capital raising, and business valuation services to growing and market-leading businesses.

Jon has approximately 20 years of merger and acquisition, strategic advisory, and business valuation experience and has successfully advised clients across a broad range of industries, including manufacturing, business services, technology, consumer and industrial products, and health care. He has closed over $2 billion in aggregate transaction value in his career.

Mr. Taylor earned his B.S. in Economics with concentrations in Finance and Real Estate from the Wharton School at the University of Pennsylvania and has an MBA from Georgetown University's McDonough School of Business. He is a Certified Valuation Analyst (CVA) with the National Association of Certified Valuators and Analysts (NACVA).

# INDEX

Made in the USA
Las Vegas, NV
28 March 2024

87876560R00079